Care in the Community for Young People
with Learning Disabilities

The Client's Voice

of related interest

**Group Homes and Community Integration
of Developmentally Disabled People –
Micro-Institutionalisation?**
Janice C Sinson
ISBN 1 85302 125 3

Community Care Practice and the Law
Michael Mandelstam with Belinda Schwehr
ISBN 1 85302 273 X

**Children with Special Needs
Assessment, Law and Practice –
Caught in the Acts, 3rd Edition**
John Friel
ISBN 1 85302 280 2

**Young Adults with Special Needs
Assessment, Law and Practice –
Caught in the Acts**
John Friel
ISBN 1 85302 231 4

Care in the Community for Young People with Learning Disabilities
The Client's Voice

Janice Sinson

Jessica Kingsley Publishers
London and Bristol, Pennsylvania

First published in the United Kingdom in 1995 by
Jessica Kingsley Publishers Ltd
116 Pentonville Road
London N1 9JB, England
and
1900 Frost Road, Suite 101
Bristol, PA 19007, U S A

Library of Congress Cataloging in Publication Data
A CIP catalogue record for this book is available
from the Library of Congress

British Library Cataloguing in Publication Data
Sinson, Janice C
Care in the Community for Young People
with Learning Disabilites:Client's
Voice
I.Title
362.350835

ISBN 1–85302–310–8

Printed and Bound in Great Britain by
Athenaeum Press, Gateshead, Tyne and Wear

Contents

In memory of Herbert Gunzburg (1914–1994)
whose work was a constant inspiration to those of us struggling
to find a way through the maze of *'mental deficiency'*, and a
powerful influence in achieving the reform that has enabled the
people in these pages to take their place in society.

Introduction

In 1992 the author reported on a unique educational venture at Wentwood, a residential sixth form college for adolescents with learning disabilities. Wentwood only accepted students below IQ50 who had previously attended special schools and the majority of students had measured IQs between 30 and 46. The two year course was not intended to provide vocational training but aimed more specifically towards providing a measure of personal competence that would enable students to join the wider community as confident independent young adults.

The report looked at the intake of the first ten years of the college and charted the progress of the 63 students from their very modest base line assessments on entry, to their final leaving achievements. During the two years at college the majority of students had learned to live fairly independent lives in a small house, travelled around the area using different forms of public transport, lived as rent paying lodgers with local families and undertaken a number of work experience projects in the community. They had learned to take advantage of local provisions such as the library, sports centre, churches, theatres, public houses and restaurants. Students attended local clubs and classes, cycled, walked, went horse riding and grew in confidence as they demonstrated their ability to live an ordinary life within an ordinary community. Their progress was set against a comparable adult sample in Scotland who used the same assessment methodology over the same period of time. The full assessment methodology, results and statistical treatment of this research can be found in Sinson (1992) and Stainton (1992). Full details of the Wentwood curriculum, which was derived from and ran alongside an on-going assessment model, can be found in the Appendix.

This book looks at how 40 of these 63 students had subsequently fared in the community and how well they had been served by the unique curriculum. Although attempts were made to contact the 63 ex-students by letter, several were living abroad, two had died, some were living in such remote parts of the British Isles that visits were not financially viable, and other letters were returned to sender. The 40, not only traced but also accessible, ex-students proved to be a representative sample of the total by virtue of age, sex, ability

1

and living environment. Several were found to have been living relatively independent lives for up to eight years, well before the advent of the Care in the Community Act.

Wherever they were now living; ex-students, their families and staff responsible for those living in group homes were interviewed by the author. During the interview the final Wentwood assessment was updated to give a clear picture of the progress of each student over the intervening years. Every ex-student had signed or marked a form agreeing to the visit and to talking about their life since leaving Wentwood. A further phone call nearer the time reminded them of the visit and confirmed they were still happy to take part. During the interview everybody answered the same questions and was encouraged to talk about anything else that seemed relevant. The interview lasted as long as the ex-student wished and very often it was possible spend part of the day accompanying people on routine shopping trips or observing how they coped with their housework and other aspects of their daily life.

Most visits lasted 2–3 hours but some extended over the day and into the evening when two or three Wentwood ex-students were living together. All the interviews were recorded on tape with the interviewee having control of the tape recorder. The majority of people appeared familiar with electronic devices and often pointed out when the batteries were failing – halting proceedings until they had been changed! There was no set format for visits to parents or staff, who all gave permission for their conversation to be recorded. These open ended discussions usually confirmed that the information given by ex-students was accurate. Parents welcomed the opportunity to talk about their gratitude to Wentwood and an almost unanimous phrase occurred – '*Wentwood gave him/her his/her independence*'.

The sample was found to represent families from all walks of life, mainly living in the Wentwood catchment area of Wiltshire, Berkshire and Avon. Visits were also made to London, Canterbury, Exeter and the Midlands. The average age of the 19 men and 21 women ex-students was 25 years, with a main range of 20–28 years. Two women of 32 years who were rather more handicapped than the main sample, and had attended Wentwood at a later age, were not included in the age range calculations as they were found to have made very little comparable progress to the main sample. Fortuitously for the statistical treatment, at the time of the interviews there were three more or less equal groups of students divided between those who were living in the family home, Group Homes and those living independent lives with differing degrees of support. There was little difference in age or ability between the groups and, as shown in the text, skill gains and losses since leaving Wentwood also conformed to these three groups. Post Wentwood, people still living in the family home had lost substantially more life skills than those living in the other two groups.[1]

Chapters 1 and 2 look at the environments in which people live. Those living in group homes describe their life as they see it, as do the staff and keyworkers involved with them. Parents also talk about the differing provisions and their concern about the time when they will no longer be there to oversee the care of their offspring. The people who still live in the family home and have lost many life skills highlight the plus and minus benefits of their more sheltered existence, as do their parents. Some of the more disturbing lifestyles are also highlighted by those people who are living relatively independently as they talk about their lives with clarity and insight.

A surprising finding during the interviews was that over half of the sample were involved in full time waged work and full, or part time, work experience within their local community with three people having recently given up such work for a variety of reasons. This percentage was not composed only of the most academically able Wentwood leavers but also included the least able. Chapter 3 looks at the lives of 'the workers' while the case study of Lizzie in Chapter 5 charts the progress of the least able Wentwood student who is now a highly skilled waged worker.

A disturbing finding of this research was that a group of the ex-students were reluctant to mix in any way with their learning disabled peers and were consequently cut off from much available social life. Through their words and that of their concerned families, the implications of this type of social isolation, and the consequent alienation, is explored in Chapter 4.

There are no conventional conclusions to this type of research and Chapter 6 merely highlights some of the salient points. Certainly readers will find others within their own experience. Unlike the majority of research reports, the main text contains no references to previously published books or papers. This is a consequence of the nature of the work which consists of transcripts of verbatim reports from people with learning disabilities living, with varying degrees of difficulty, in the community. There is no way in which their experiences can be validated or confirmed by reference to previous findings and there is nothing to be gained by seeking to show that such findings are consensual with the prevailing view of the scientific community. The findings reported are *sui generis* data and provide a unique insight into the lives of people who, only now, are finding a visible place in our communities. To help set their lives in the context of current thought a list of further reading is appended. In this text the clients speak for themselves and it is through their words and their eyes that we see care in the community.

---

1   The full statistical treatment and results of this research can be obtained from the British Society for Developmental Disabilities who part funded a proportion of the data collection.

CHAPTER 1

The Group Home

Much has been written by professionals involved in transition and relocation into community living. This chapter will try to present a somewhat different unified perspective of the views of staff, families and residents. It would appear from this research that the sticking point of all community care policies from the point of view of the protagonists is the ambivalence of people with developmental disabilities, who clearly express needs for simultaneous independence and dependence. To confuse the issue further this is combined with a demand for continuing emotional support. Rather than fragment this concept, a format has been adopted allowing the reader to explore the differing problems. As each person is uniquely different, so were their expressed needs and lifestyles – making policy and planning very difficult.

The life stories illustrated below cover the most common areas of need in the group home setting. The Wentwood sample was more or less equally divided between the three types of living units which they regarded as home. Thirty per cent still lived in the family home, 37 per cent in group homes and 33 per cent were living relatively independent lives in what they regarded as their home in the community. The fact that skill gains or losses since leaving Wentwood conformed to these three differing environments suggests that, post Wentwood, the environment is as significant a factor in further development as was the initial curriculum. **Those ex-students who had gone on to group homes after leaving Wentwood had retained their teaching and gained more new life skills than those who had stayed within the family home.**

There was a clear trend for new group homes to be small houses in suburban streets and only 15 per cent of the entire sample lived in houses of more than six people. It was interesting to note that of the 70 per cent of the sample living away from home, 46 per cent of these were living with other ex-Wentwood students. Three ex-students, who had lived together for eight years, had progressed through a larger group home to a semi-independent self contained flat for six people. This accounted for three people living in larger units. The percentage of residents in the various sizes of group home is shown in the diagram.

Group homes are defined, regardless of size, as staffed units where ex-students were not living a fully independent life and were involved in

Living Unit Size

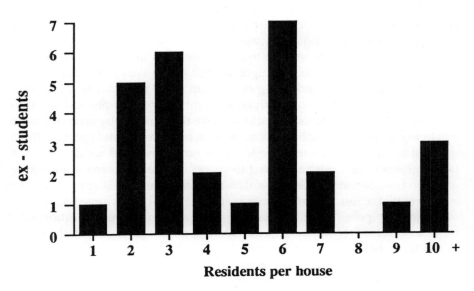

Figure 1. Percentage of residents in various sizes of group home

semi-communal living. Twelve different group homes were visited and there was little similarity between them, although the problems of the residents were common to them all. In the larger group homes most of the sample were living in small units or training flats and were amongst the most independent of the residents. Without exception, for the Wentwood ex-students, these were happy places where they enjoyed full and active social lives.

People had as much contact as they chose with their families although in many cases the parents would have liked more contact. There were signs of a shift away from the family home as, even in the smaller units, residents often preferred to stay in the group home for weekends and Christmas to be involved in the enjoyable communal life. Residents belonged to the usual clubs and made good use of all the sporting facilities available for people with developmental disabilities. Friends of either sex were welcomed and where people were independent travellers they moved about their local area quite freely. People went out to work, work experience, further education colleges and various adult centres.

Bedrooms were individually furnished with a wealth of electronic wizardry in the form of computers, music centres, televisions, video cameras and video machines. One room housed a full scale drum kit. Only three people shared rooms. Two ladies, both in otherwise good independent group homes, shared rooms in somewhat cramped conditions. They appeared to be quite content with the situation, as were their parents. A gentleman shared his room with his fiancée as part of an admirable forward looking policy in a MENCAP group home. Unfortunately, parents are far less happy with this type of policy and there were no signs of similar policies in local authority group homes. Some group homes did not allow members of the opposite sex in bedrooms.

However, it would be unwise to generalise from this particular well adjusted sample. They had been taught, as part of the Wentwood curriculum, that leaving the family and living away from home was part of the natural progression into adulthood and those resident in group homes had asked to go there. Those ex-students who did not take this philosophy on board were still living in the family home as were those whose parents did not wish them to leave home. There were other less able non-Wentwood residents in the larger group homes who appeared to spend most of their free time sitting glued to the ubiquitous television. The lives of these people appeared to be similar to that of residents of the group homes cited in a previous study where such places imposed on the residents a subtle form of micro-institutionalisation. Sinson (1992) found most of the catering, cleaning, laundry and gardening in these homes was covered by domestic or contract staff with special arrangements being made for the few more independent residents living in the smaller units. Every ex-Wentwood group home resident spent time at home each week doing their domestic chores and usually shopped independently and prepared the evening meal during this time.

Tom and John
For the last eight years Tom, aged 28, and John, aged 27, had lived in a fully staffed MENCAP group home for seven residents. A modernised house, in a street of identical houses, it was one and a half miles from the town with adequate public transport enabling all the residents to walk or travel independently by bus to wherever they wished to go. Tom's parents lived within walking distance in a similar street – as had John's until recently. On their retirement they moved from the area and to their deep disappointment John chose to stay in the group home. The house had been recently refurbished and the residents temporarily relocated which had led to a certain amount of emotional and physical disruption. Both Tom and John had good jobs in the town which they had held for several years.

John
John was one of the least able ex-students and had reached a far lower final assessment skill level than the majority of students. Nevertheless he had increased his skills over the years and travelled independently to his job in a photographic company. His communication ability was limited and he had a physical disability which made walking difficult for him.

The house was adequately staffed but the staff appeared very short of time and rather more stressed than in many other group homes. The pleasant garden was well kept by staff with little sign of the residents helping. Staff were responsible for bulk shopping and laundry but the residents spent half a day a week at home learning to shop, prepare the evening meal and clean their rooms.

Tom and Jill

Tom shared his room with his diabetic fiancée, Jill, to whom he had recently became engaged. They both have Down's syndrome. As he matured over the years Tom had retained all his Wentwood teaching and increased his post Wentwood assessment by a creditable 18 life skills. Happy to talk about his life, the interview took place in his shared bedroom, of which he was very proud. Regardless of his stammer he tried hard to communicate and enjoyed using the tape recorder.

Do you see your family much? Yes. *When do you see them?* Here and Mum's house. *Does your Mum live here* – not far off – *do you know her phone number because I'd like to go and see her* – [Rattles off phone number and address].

Do you and Jill go out a lot together? Yes. *Who buys your clothes?* I do. *Where do you get the money from?* I'm not sure. *Who gives you the money?* Staff.

Every second Tuesday, that's once a fortnight is my sports club. Friday is club night at the Baptist church and I go on a bus with my bus pass until 31st March 1994. I work hard and we're going to get engaged together.

When? I have done. *Has she got a ring?* Yes. *Did you buy the ring?* Yes. *Did you go and choose it with her?* I did. *Where did you get it from?*

Jersey. Jersey on holiday – just me and Jill and a staff from here.

What did you do in Jersey? Quite a lot. We were flying in an aeroplane from London Heathrow – *and where did you stay* [rattles off full address] we had dinner in the evenings –

And what did Jill like? She liked being with me! *Did she. She's the right sort of girl friend to have!*

Are you going to get married? I'm living with her – *are you?* Yes. *When will you get married?* Someday – *and where will you live when you get married?* Hertfordshire. *Where abouts?* I don't know.

Why do you want to get married? I do – *but why* – its nice as you are isn't it? *That's a very small bed, is it big enough for the two of you?* It's a double.

Do you go to church? Yes it's not far away. *How often do you go?* On special occasions like Christmas day and special times and that.

you do all week – do you go to the centre? No *Where do you go?* Work
's. What time does Jill come home from the centre?

...... four. I do the shopping every Thursday it's my day off – I'm
cooking today.

What are you going to do tonight? Me and Jill might go to the cinema
somewhere. *Who do you go with?* Only the two of us.

Where do you get the money from? Staff. *Do you keep money on you?* Yes. *You've
got money there on the table haven't you?* It's not mine it's Jill's.

What are those cups? Darts and snooker. *Who won them?* We did, me and Jill
– *did you, where?* At Monday club.

What else should I know about you I got- I got -I got a nnn--ew- I got a neww-
v - *video?*

> No I got a new volunteer from s-s-school boys and he takes me out
> somewhere. He's not starting till next month – the end of September.

*So you've got a volunteer who comes. Does he take you out during the day or at
night?* Yes day – *and did you have one last year?* Yes. *Was he nice?* Not really.
Why not? I don't know I didn't like him much.

What do you like doing best? The video machine. *Did you buy it?* No Jill's sister
– she give it to us by a cheque. *Can you work all this yourself?* Yes – more than
I can.

*If you're unhappy – like when you didn't like your volunteer and you were unhappy
– who do you tell?* [silence] *what do you do?* Ann knows about that.

So you tell Ann do you? I always tell her. *Do you tell Jill if you're unhappy?* No.
What makes you unhappy? I don't know. *Are you ever unhappy?* Yes. Ann
knows, ask Ann.

Would you like me to ask Ann? Yes. *Is Ann the only person you talk to?* She's
always around.

Do you tell your Mum if you're unhappy?

[Tom gets very angry and starts shouting and stammering and after some
effort gets the sentence out.]

> Just Ann and not my Mum. She's worse she puts it on me and nagging
> too much most of the time

Your Mum nags does she? Yes. *Does she nag all the time?* Yes most of the time.
Does she nag your sister too? Yes she does. *Has she always nagged?* Yes she does
always.

You like going home – not all the time. *You're happy here are you?* Yes. *What
about your sister does she nag you?* No. *What does mum nag you about?* Ann

knows about that. *Does your Mum treat you like a little boy – not an adult?* Yes Ann knows.

Tom became distressed and started stammering and pointing to the tape recorder. He refused an offer to turn it off. He had been holding it himself, having been asked if he minded it running, and had demonstrated that it recorded what we were saying and appeared to enjoy playing it back.

I want to talk to the machine with Ann

What do you want to talk to me about? [silence] *Does your mum know about it?* She knows about it.

Would you rather your Mother didn't know? She told me that.

Who told you that? My Mum – ask Ann about it.

On Tom's insistence we went to the office to find Ann (the house manager) explaining that Tom wanted to talk into the machine about something but it was not clear what. Ann was very welcoming at the end of a long day during which she had been tied up in meetings. She was also probably off duty and more than ready to go home. It subsequently transpired that the events Tom wished to recount had happened some time before Ann had been in post but she knew a little about them. It would have been very easy for her to either cover them up or suggest to Tom that they were not really the sort of thing to tell visitors about. Tom's speech impediment would have ensured that it was almost impossible to discover what he was talking about. In the face of his obvious distress and confronted with a complete stranger she had not met before, she handled the situation impeccably. Tom's responses are printed in bold type in the exchange below.

Now then tell me what it is you want to tell me about with Ann and the machine. Was it the volunteer from school you wanted me to ask Ann about... very long silence.

ANN: I can hear what you're saying Tom... [long silence – then tears]...

There was a man who worked here that you didn't like? Yes. Because he did things you didn't like or said things you didn't like? **Said things and the other one Paul he had it.**

Paul won't come again because we've asked him never to come to the house again. Alf was the one that worked here and Paul was a volunteer friend. Alf was dismissed wasn't he and you made some statements didn't you – what you thought about the things that you didn't like. The things that offended you and made you feel angry, mocked at, frustrated, and your feelings felt hurt. Both Alf and Paul have left now – Alf resigned and May had to leave – they were two members of staff.

And what was it they were doing Tom? **I can't remember.**

ANN: You can't remember what they did, can you remember how you felt about it... [silence]

Were you here then, Ann? No.

ANN: Does your Mum know what they did, Tom – how they behaved? It has upset you hasn't it, Tom [sobs hopelessly] *He kept saying he wanted me to talk to you about it. It's all right Tom we all get upset specially when people do things to us and we don't like it* [sobs]

ANN: Your Mum knew that they left. Did she know what they did, Tom? Did she know how they spoke to people or how they behaved? How they behaved to you?

[long and incomprehensible mumble that Ann seemed to make some sense of. Odd words like manager and staff were clear]

ANN: That's right. Barry was the manager here and Eve was the area manager and they went up to national headquarters and you made them some statements, didn't you. You told all the people what had happened. That was very brave of you. They had a court case, didn't they, and you really helped. It helped them to hear what happened and how you felt about it. That must have helped everybody and then it couldn't have happened again once you'd told them. Alf and May won't be employed here again and Paul won't be a volunteer.

Was he the volunteer from school? No.

ANN: Was that another volunteer you didn't like Tom? **Yes.**

Did you have any other things that you wanted to tell Janice about or any thoughts or feelings that you wanted to talk about with Janice? **Not really.**

We were talking quite nicely about darts championships and work and going on the bus before all this started! I wanted to hear about how he helped Jill who he said was diabetic.

ANN: I think Tom and Jill personally do well to travel independently. Don't you Tom? They're very much independent and do their own thing. They've just recently moved into that double room haven't you? Tom and Jill have been really delighted to be in that double room. Tell Janice what you are saving up for now.

A small fridge for Jill's injections she's on insulin she can't have much sugar see. *Does she inject herself?* **Yes she does – it's evenings and mornings as well.**

ANN: Tom is pretty good on the whole about encouraging Jill, particularly if we've got agency staff – Jill finds it hard to get up – or she if she has her insulin she tends to run back to bed and not eat.

And also – like Jill had last time – she had her turns and goes her sugar goes wrong and she throws about and everything goes wrong.

ANN: She gets cross and shouts doesn't she – **and also about Jill's periods.** What about Jill's periods?

It's due – it's bad

I think perhaps we're going to the GP and perhaps evening primrose oil might help her with the aches that she gets.

Do you look after Jill when she has her period? **I always do.** *What sort of things do you do?* **Make her a hot cup of tea, hot bottle.**

ANN: You're a great chap Tom. He's a really thoughtful chap – he's really good at anticipating when staff need a cup of tea, and also often when everyone else is in he and Jill clear everything up and then make a drink for everyone completely unasked. What about when you have your house meeting on Wednesday? They have a house meeting – what do you talk about?

Lots of things – role play.

ANN: They've only had two sessions. The first one you came to but closed your eyes but you said you could hear everything. The second one you decided not to come to – you were not too sure about it were you Tom? I don't think you were alone, I think there were other people here who weren't feeling too sure about what might go on.

One of the things I found when I first came here was that there was lots of underlying anxieties and anger about having a whole big staffing change. We'd also been closed for refurbishing. Two very big changes and as time went on there was an awful lot of getting at one another – wasn't there? Everybody living here was getting at one another and they had staff that they didn't really know. My feeling was that they'd been here eight years and they'd lost staff they knew and had four new staff.

[Tom departs happily to help make the evening meal]

They went on holiday to Jersey with Sue. Although she had worked with them for some time before she was quite surprised at the amount of input that was needed for Tom and Jill. She thought that they would do things in the day together and they would choose where they would like to go. In the evening, because there was a bar on the premises and other activities going on, she thought they would probably want to take themselves off after dinner to those activities, and that she could have a break. Even an hour's break. But she found they were standing outside her bedroom door waiting for her to come down and be alongside.

Although they seem very independent and have practised over a period of time – they are independent travellers – Tom goes to work on the bus. Somewhere strange or if something that is not predictable arises, there is difficulty dealing with it. Like all of us it's practice that makes us more able people.

When I first came here I was told that there was a lot of very able independent people here but in fact they weren't. We were having difficulties and people were not getting to day centre on time. Now they choose their own bedtime and they are getting to work on tine. They've worked through a lot of things – but when I first came I was told they were a very able group – a very happy group etc. What I actually found was that there were lots and lots of things going on.

[Interruption by Tom. Jill was having a 'turn']

ANN: Fine, what she really needs to do is drink two glasses of cold water without anything in. **Yes.** You've done that? **Yes** –

Marvellous, you can follow with a sugar free drink OK? Thank you for coming up that's great – it was good of you to communicate about that Tom because you know what's going on – I'll be down in three to five minutes, thanks Tom.

Tom seems to regard you as an emotional support. He said he wasn't very happy about his Mother; she nagged a lot. He said Ann knows – she knows all about it, ask Ann.

Yes, I do know he has been very upset. There was a time when all the staff were having a meeting and we heard this wail right from the front of the house – of pain and anguish. Everybody flew in – I didn't know what had happened – I didn't even know if it was a human being it was such a wail of anguish. Tom had been on the phone to his Mum and he'd been delighted to get through about something, and his mum had disagreed and got cross about something, and he was just so frustrated and upset.

I think she's very upset about the relationship with Jill. I think the fact that there might be a sexual relationship there. She's not sure about it and doesn't want to know even though she knew they had counselling for a sexual relationship. I don't know myself in actual fact if there's a sexual relationship or what but she's on the pill.

Tom's parents

Did Tom go there directly from Wentwood? No he came home, he was home here for a year or two.

What did you do with him at home?

> He went to the adult training centre. I was quite happy having him at home. I was quite happy actually and there was a hostel opening near by. He thought he'd like to go there – we didn't encourage him much but he still wanted to go himself you know. He wanted to go.

Would you rather have kept him at home?

> Yes and no. Now – you've got to be – have you got a lot of dealings with children with Down's syndrome? Do you understand what they're like? He's such a lovely boy one minute and the next minute you know – specially when it came to the evening time and he wanted to go out. Boys of his age want to go out and he'd say Mum and Dad let's go out somewhere – go to a pub or something. It's rarely we go to a pub. Maybe weekends we'll work in the garden or something, but he wanted to go out – and that was it.

Before he went to Wentwood was he all right?

> When he went to school. Oh yes he was all right. Then it was when he came back from Wentwood he wanted to go out.

Did he go out on his own much?

> Yes he'd go to the adult training centre on his own. This was a follow up of what they'd taught him at Wentwood. They taught him every-thing like that.

Did he go into town on his own then?

> No, just to the centre; that was as far as he'd go. If he went further I was with him. I wouldn't let him – we're too protective of those boys really, but the town is very difficult – worse than London. Wentwood was a little village really, everybody knew them. He did little jobs there didn't he? Did he tell you that?

He works now. Yes – he works now.

Does he phone much? Yes he does. *How often does he come home?* We just leave it up to himself now, whenever he wants to. He phones and says he's coming to see us – you know with Jill, because she's his girl friend as you know. Have you seen her? *Yes she came in from the centre as I left – a sweet girl. Has he had a girl friend before?* I don't think so – no –

Do you phone him and ask him for lunch on Sunday?

> No, usually he rings himself and says he's coming home Sunday. He'll have his lunch down there and come after lunch and they'll go back for a meal in the evening.

What does he do when he comes home; does he bring Jill with him? Yes, most of the time. He'll have a video to watch. *Do you get on with Jill?*

> I get on with her all right. Her talking isn't very good, not as good as Tom but his isn't very good as you know. A lot of people are saying that it's nice that Tom is there because we're retired now – his future is taken care of. His bedroom is here and I'd like him to be here but I shouldn't say that.

Do you miss him? No I don't miss him now, I did at first.

How long did you miss him for?

> He's been there eight years. For the first couple of years, that's all. But he comes home so often he's so near home. People do say to us we've done the right thing.

Do you think you've done the right thing?

> He loves it there; he'd never leave it, I'm sure. What else could he do. It's more boring at home. We haven't got the things going for him that they have in there. They're having a lovely summer's day out today aren't they? He goes to different clubs – I suppose we haven't regretted it really.

Could you ever see Tom living in a house in the community – in the new Community Care Act?

> I couldn't. I just could not. I mean it has been talked about but how could the likes of Tom go in a flat on his own without any staff? He's not well up – he copes, yes, but there's an awful lot of back up goes on. People do say 'isn't Tom great'. Tom is this or that. I mean like today, he phoned up and said they're going on a summer outing all of them with the staff – and I said where are you going Tom and he said I don't know. He has an awful habit of saying I don't know – and I said you're supposed to be a clever boy Tom by everybody. It annoys me when people say that to me about Tom. I know what Tom is. I've lived all the years with him. He has that childish way still about him. I don't know – I'm sure he must have known where they were going.

Father comes in and joins the conversation.

Are you happy with him there?

> Yes, we have to treat him as a man now and that's what he wants. He gets well looked after there – we'd rather he were at home if we had the choice, yes.

MUM: If we could have coped with him – then again we worry about that other boy. Both his parents died within a week of each other and he was just left alone and the sisters had to come in and take him to their flat. And they were always working for MENCAP, – and they were going to put him in a hostel and they kept putting it off and putting it off – and saying yes he'll go to one of these places one day. One day – and they never got around to it and they died.

DAD: They have friends there – if they had to split them up, like John, they did make an effort to take him down to where they were going when they retired – but again he wouldn't budge.

They wanted to take him?

> Oh yes, he said he liked it best there. He liked it so much he wouldn't go. What can you say – where can you find the perfect place? If we wanted to move away he'd never come with us – we'd have to leave him. It probably will happen but he wouldn't leave there – our daughter's here anyway.

If it were possible to separate out all the individual strands from the whole that makes up Tom's life with his fiancee, his parents, his work, life in the group home and relationships with his peers, each of them would probably have a complexity that would be difficult for a more able person to cope with. With his speech impediment and limited intellectual ability it is clear that Tom is reliant on the sort of emotional support he derives from knowing that, independent as he may be, a member of staff will always be available to turn to for support 24 hours a day. Yet he is able to care for and support his fiancee in an adult and responsible manner and derive great pleasure from the relationship.

Mark

MENCAP has always been a parent-orientated concern and there were signs that where staff attempted to foster independence in the residents they were often defeated by parents. Residents' money was often still controlled by parents as was much of their social life. Conversations like the one below were all too common!

Mark, aged 27, has Down's syndrome and lives with two other men, in a semi-independent MENCAP flat on top of a large hostel. His life is centred round MENCAP Gateway and other MENCAP functions and the club house is just across the road from the hostel. Staff take the residents out and ensure they have a good social life. He goes to college three days a week and has worked at McDonalds two days a week for three years, travelling to both independently by bus. Either staff or family handle all his money and buy his clothes. In the face of such a sheltered lifestyle he had managed to retain all his Wentwood teaching and post-Wentwood had acquired a creditable further 13 life skills.

His parents are in their seventies and bring him home to stay every weekend and although they have other children their life is centred round him. They expressed their views about Mark's other home during one of these weekends. Similar views about MENCAP were held by other parents.

Mark had reasonable communication skills and an unusually light and pleasant voice but still needed an interpreter for much of what he said. His mother terminated the interview, saying that Mark was getting bored and couldn't concentrate for long. The interview was a four way conversation and it was difficult to talk to Mark on his own. However, in a short time alone with him looking at all his possessions in his bedroom, much of what he said confirmed the information given by his parents. The extract below was part of the interview with Mark's parents and in the light of their obvious devotion to their son the father's feelings were very sad and indicated the burden of guilt shared by many parents in this research.

Parents

> The money comes here because his Mum's an appointee – we get it out, pay it into the building society and once a month we then pay MEN-CAP.

You handle it all?

> He needs bus fare even with a pass. When he goes on a bus he's always got to have a 10p piece on him. Wherever he goes he pays 10p. Staff give it to him. The DSS pay to us £249 a week. £225 a week has to go to the hostel that is for his board, living, clothes, personal allowance and disability allowance. Everybody pays it the way that they choose. There's not many are appointees – about seven of us. He has £5 a week pocket money and puts that in a box in his drawer and he uses a pound a day. He's supposed to go in the office for any other money he wants.

So he keeps £5 a week of his own?

> Yes and I don't want to know what he spends it on. I wouldn't trust him with money. They don't do shopping on their own for food, only with staff. Mostly the food is brought in bulk and they go down to the kitchen and get the loaf and milk for their breakfast – and the food to cook for the evening meal.

At one time they were going to buy their own food and cook their evening meal themselves – but they were in such chaos that we said 'Look – either you are going to feed him or we're going to bring him home and feed him.' Sometimes they go out without breakfast – but that's their fault because they haven't got up early enough to do it. For lunch they take sandwiches. They have to do the sandwiches the night before. Then at night now, they come home and they have certain jobs to do. They're on a rota and they get help to cook a proper meal.

Father

Does he have a key-worker?

Yes but she only does four hours a week and its not enough because they are all only part time workers – its a failing. If they're going to split them up into small groups there should be someone they can turn to like a house mother. You send boys off to a boarding school and there is definitely a matron they can turn to because they regard her as responsible. They usually all respond to a female person where they can go if there's tears coming. This is a failing of the present system – that they have no-one. They should have someone to go to.

When you have Down's you're not told what to do. We realise now they've got to be pushed right from square one. I don't believe that if you knew that you were carrying a Down's child that you should continue. Given an ideal society – OK – but the society that we live in does not accept them – and its every inch of the way you're battling to keep things. It's the same with lots of people in wheel chairs, what chance have they got? They're going out and around if they've got parents alive, yes. Some of those in the MENCAP hostel where he is now, they'll never get any more out of life because they haven't got parents to back them up. MENCAP used to be more for looking after young people – now they employ so many people on a shift basis there's no continuity.

You don't think the staff themselves are able to do this?

No. MENCAP House where he is now used to be lovely. They used to have a lady and she was the mother. They'd go over to the club across the road and she'd go and fetch them and take them back home. She was a house mother and they loved her. Now there's about 25 staff – sitting in the office. They leave before you find out their name.

Lily

In another MENCAP group home the following conversation occurred with Lily, aged 24, a very smart loquacious young lady with Down's syndrome who was dark, vivacious and thin with a very fashionable hair style. Her

interview indicated her dependence on the staff who were really only periph-
erally involved with her life. She lived independently with three other people,
in a flat which was one of several on the site for people with varying degrees
of dependence. Some residents needed round the clock care, so part of the
unit was fully staffed, which ensured that someone was always available on
the internal phone system. All the parents lived in the town, and being a
parent operated concern, there were both pluses and minuses as interviews
with parents and the director revealed.

Lily wore high heels and a tight fashionable navy skirt with a spotless white
blouse. Having just returned from work she changed out of her working
clothes and was wearing her interview clothes! She looked sophisticated,
controlled and very self-possessed. Some of her speech was difficult to
understand (and equally difficult to transcribe from tape) but she repeated
things carefully and patiently. She was possibly the most truly independent
person in the entire sample, even though she was living in a group home.

All housekeeping money was controlled by MENCAP with Lily's flat
getting a weekly allowance for food but, as seen in Chapter 3, she went to
work daily and had control of personal finances. She did her own shopping
and knew all her clothes sizes. The other three people in the flat were also
independent but they chose to join in the main group home communal life to
go to outside social events – usually those run by MENCAP and Gateway.

There were no ambivalences about Lily's situation. She appeared in control
of her life and showed the interviewer everything in her flat with a running
commentary on where she bought things and what she spent. She went to the
dentist on her own but preferred to be taken to the doctor by staff. She saw
her parents weekly but found them a bit of a bind and hadn't quite learned
to deal with the situation tactfully. According to the staff this lead to her
parents being hurt sometimes.

She was encouraged by the manager of the home to go to local self-advocacy classes with other residents one evening a week, but as the conversation
progressed it was clear she had no real understanding of the concept and what
the classes were for. She was, however, most enthusiastic about the social side
of the evening.

A member of staff usually shared the evening meal in the flat but the four
flatmates cooked everything themselves. The staff member was there to
ensure that the meal was a pleasant social event and to monitor any problems
that may have arisen during the day. MENCAP provided a full social life for
everybody with varied holidays of their choice and even an annual dinner
dance that the residents went to with their club, not their families. Whatever
the residents lost in independence or freedom by living on the fringes of a
fully staffed institution was compensated for by the stability and companion-
ship they all obviously enjoyed. They had little contact with the other flats for
people of higher dependency and it was clear that Lily was happy most of the

time with the level of control applied to her life and free time – and possibly needed that extra security of knowing someone would always be available if needed.

Do you ever go to any pubs? No. *You don't go there with anyone?* No. *Shopping?* Yes I do. *Who do you go shopping with?* By myself. *Do you buy your food?* Yes we all go to Sainsbury's once a week and do a big shop.

Who cooks the food? All of us. *What do you have for breakfast?* Cereal and toast. *Does somebody help you make it?* No we do it ourselves. *What will you have for lunch today?* Sandwiches – *are they already made?* No I make them myself.

Are the others in for lunch? No only me. *What about your meal tonight?* I'm cooking tonight. *What are you having?* Pork chops, I put the pork chops out ready last night. *Are they frozen?* Yes. *How will you cook them?* Under the grill. *What will you have with with them?* Potatoes, celery, tomatoes. *Do you cook all this yourself?* Yes. *Are you going to have any pudding?* No.

Do you ever go shopping yourself? Yes, I walk in when I've finished work and then I walk back. *Do you ever go out for coffee in town?* Yes we do.

Do you go to church? Yes, every Sunday. *Who with?* My parents. *Have you any friends that don't live here?* No. *Have you got any friends where Mum and Dad live?* No. All my friends are here.

This is your home isn't it? Yes. *How often do you go to your Mum and Dad's?* I get a lift every Sunday and I have lunch and tea and go to church.

Would you rather live here or with your Mum and Dad? I'd rather live here.

If you're unhappy here or at work or you have an argument who do you tell? No-one. *No-one?* Never no. *Do you tell your Mum and Dad?* I said no.

Do you tell the staff here? Sometimes. *Sometimes or always?* Sometimes. *Usually you don't tell anybody?* No. *Do you have arguments with the others in the flat?* No, we get on well.

Is there anything you can't do that you want to do? I can't go horse-riding. *Do you want to go horse-riding?* Yes I do *Where would you go?* The stables – I used to go to. *And you'd like to go again?* I can't go. *Why not, have you asked Pat* [her key-worker]. She isn't here in the afternoons. They go in the afternoon.

What's this [looking at poster on wall]. A group. *A self-advocacy group?* Yes. *What do you do there?* We talk and have a drink there.

What do you talk about? All sorts of things – I don't know. *Is it about speaking up for yourself and saying what you want?* Yes, that's right, yes.

Could you ask them to help you ask to go riding? No – staff won't let me go.

The interviewer asked both the key-worker and the house manager if there was any objection to Lily going riding – especially as one of her flatmates was taken by minibus each Saturday because the stables were in the country and not on a direct bus route. They seemed genuinely surprised that she hadn't mentioned she wanted to go and could see no reason why she shouldn't.

Jane and Alan

Jane and Alan lived in a well established group home for 12 adults run by a private housing association affiliated to a religious foundation. The old Georgian house and garden were well sited in the middle of the city, giving the residents easy access to shops, parks, bus routes, further education establishments, sporting and entertainment facilities. There was a strong religious faith within the house and links with a charity that provided schools and homes for all ages and types of disability. The charity ran a contact group for families with children or adults with mental handicap and held weekly evening prayer meetings. The foundation also organised visits to Lourdes, holidays and other social events within the local community.

The two senior staff in the group home had been in post for nine and six years. The two ex-students Jane and Alan, both aged 27, had been well settled there for five years. The home fostered communal living but Alan had recently moved into the integral flat for two people which offered rather more personal independence. People seemed reluctant to segregate themselves, as the communal life appeared to be enjoyed by all the residents. There was some similarity between the happy bustling atmosphere in the home and that of Wentwood. Jane and Alan travelled independently to work and college and both had retained and expanded their Wentwood repertoire of skills. It was interesting that Jane, who left Wentwood with a relatively modest final score, had gained two further skills and lost two so retained the same overall score. Alan, who had a low final Wentwood assessment had gained a total of 28 life skills and was now of a comparable developmental level to Jane. He had gained in maturity and was contemplating a more independent lifestyle than Jane would probably be capable of. Alan had not returned home to stay with his family since arriving at the home but Jane attended the weekly evening prayer and social meeting with her mother. She slept at home and returned to the group home the next morning.

Life was happy, but money appeared short and everyone had worked hard over the years to save and budget for a better standard of living, as the manager explained when talking about Alan and Jane's lives. The first topic to be discussed was the ever problematic financial situation, this time compounded by a general shortage of money in the home. Jane was interviewed before the house manager and most of what she said was confirmed by the house manager's interview. Jane remained in the room during the house manager's interview. Although no-one in the house would dream of violating her privacy during her interview, equally, when she was being talked about it was taken for granted that she would be present to hear what was said. Alan chose not to join in as he had 'flu and decided to get up late that day.

House manager

> *Do you give Jane all her £12?*

No. I encourage them to save because they usually spend it all in one go. One pound won't buy anything – so she can take her money if she wants because it is her money. But I normally aim to save about £5 a week as that buys them clothes. She's got a Post Office book which I keep and a budget book which I write up for them. When they were stolen, it was a good job I kept their account number – to be honest with you there's a lot of money in their books now.

Like the others, when Jane first came she hardly had any money – the whole £10 was spent on her toiletries and activities when she first came. So she never had savings behind her. If they wanted to go and buy anything there wasn't the money there and it used to sadden me – so I decided we had to save. Now, if she wanted a colour TV or she wanted a bike she's got the money there to go and buy anything. It's a great achievement. Jane's bought her bike – Alan has bought his bike and they've bought their hammocks and televisions for their room and they've done what **they** want. It's a great achievement for them. With Jane it was always second hand clothes – now she has new clothes.

I have to encourage her to spend her own money. She knows she could come and ask me tomorrow for a watch – she wants a new watch – and that I'd give her the money to go and buy it. She goes along to the PO and gets the money. I ask her how much she wants and she says £5 usually. I say that's not going to be enough, Jane, you want a bit more so she asks for another £5 and eventually we get to £20. I write the £20 in the book because you've got to write it in words – and she signs it and takes it along to the Post Office. I don't go with her.

We've got a special safe. They get their book and then they go along and get it out of the Post Office and bring it back. Then we put their pocket money in their own accounts. We had three burglaries and we lost an awful lot of money so we have to be very careful – so we have to put it all away straight away. We actually write their personal allowance in their book. Jane is allocated a specific amount a day to try and get her to budget her money. Fifty pence a day pocket money to try and give her encouragement to budget. She used to get it Monday, Wednesday and Friday – but she goes out more so the pound she'll have on a Monday will have to last her three days and the pound on Thursday, five days.

We give her a strip of bus tickets so that she'll have them if she wants them. Her job is quite hard to get to – she's got to go through the city and catch a bus to go to the other side – and she'll really do it without problems.

Don't their parents send any money?

No. Not a lot of them do. It's a tragedy – I don't know. It's as if they're cut off. They're in care, very strange. We've been saving up desperately to try and get a holiday this year. It's quite hard to raise the money and we've been raising money for two years hoping to go on holiday next year.

What happens in the summer? Jane's mother takes her away to Butlins. *What are you going to do at Christmas – are they going to stay here?* They always do I can't get rid of them on Christmas Day.

Don't their parents want them home? Yes, but they won't go!

Do they all choose to stay for Christmas?

Yes, if they don't want to go home they don't go home. The parents get very upset. Alan has never gone home since he's been here. He will never go home whatever's going on. Last Christmas 120 turned up. I give them a Christmas party on the 15th Dec and they can invite everybody.

And on Christmas Day do you invite people?

Yes, but parents can come in any time; we never ever turn people away – anyone can come in at any time – that's what we are about – most people's parents come here about once a week or so.

(JANE: **I made a Christmas cake** – *did you – did you cook it yourself?*)

No what happens is I make a great big Christmas cake and I mix it here – so that they can all wish – and then I take it home and cook it through the night. Then I take one of them to sleep at home with me to take it out of the oven and we bring it back.

Who does the cleaning? They do their own rooms. *What about the bathroom?*

We've got a domestic because it's such a big house. What happens is one day a week they're all allocated to the domestic and we've also got duty lists. Jane helps with the toilet.

Who cleans this lounge?

We all muck in if it needs doing we all do it. If Jane's got nothing to do she'll go and put the hoover over here won't you Jane? She's good at housework.

Who does the cooking?

They take a packed lunch normally to work. They have sandwiches because we cook one evening meal and they all have that together. They love it because that's the time they are together. What happened was because everyone did different things on different days, we weren't really knowing what they were having for lunch. If they take sandwiches and have a cooked meal when they come home in the evening, you know what they were eating.

Who makes the cooked meal? Staff do, we have tea about five o'clock.

What about weekends?

What we sometimes do is I prepare the vegetables and staff help them with the cooking but their concentration is not that reliable. Alan is just beginning to get his breakfast and he'll steadily go on to get his own meals. If they want to make beans on toast if they're in instead of sandwiches at lunch time, they can manage that. Jane can bake: she's marvellous at sponges.

Everything here is theirs that they can have – they know I'd never restrict them. But they're so rigid and structured it's weird. Breakfast is like clockwork – everyone the same. They do breakfast at 8 o'clock every morning. If she's here, Jane has coffee about 10 o'clock or half past and then dinner at 12 o'clock – don't we Jane? Because we have a severe diabetic we have to be really structured about our meal times. The other thing is getting them all out in the morning. They've all get to leave by half past eight. Jane doesn't usually eat between meals – some of the others make a coffee – she's more like me – I don't eat between meals.

Can they use the phone?

They've got their own phone which is a pay phone and parents ring in on that one and they answer that one. Jane is incredible about birthdays. If a member of staff has a birthday she'll come down on her own to the pay-phone and she rings them to sing Happy Birthday. They all remember every birthday.

Do they do any gardening?

Oh yes – I bought them a safety plug so that you can leave them unattended. They used to tangle up the wires and I'd stand there cringing! They do all the gardening now – Jane helps with the gardening when she comes back.

They like a cooked breakfast on a Saturday, and we can't be doing it in rotation – we have it about 8.30 to 9.30. On Sundays they sometimes get up and have their breakfast and go back to sleep. With Jane because she's frightened she's going to miss anything she gets up early.

Alan

Alan was happy to talk about his life whilst we looked at the flat he shares with his friend James.

Do you ever go to the pub? Yes sometimes with my girlfriend Alice. *Where do you go?* The Peel – *Round here?* Yes I walk down. Alice lives at home and she works in Littlewoods.

Where did you meet her? At Gateway club. *How often do you see her?* Monday, Tuesday, Wednesday at college, Thursday and Saturdays. *Does your girl friend come here?* Yes. *Do you go to church?* Yes on Sunday night with James. He shares with me here in the flat. *Is that a different church?* Yes. *You don't go with the others?* No with James. *Have you any hobbies?*

I used to go riding at Wentwood. I used to do judo a lot there but I don't do it any more.

Did you like that? Yes – I don't do that any more. *Would you like to to do judo now?* I don't have time see – I'm too busy to fit it in.

Is it better here or at Wentwood? I like them both. I liked it at Wentwood where I cooked for myself. *Do you cook for yourself here in the flat?* Not yet. *But you did cook at Wentwood. Will you like it better when you cook here?* Yes.

Who decides when you go to bed? I just tell them when I go to bed. *How do you get up in the morning?* I get myself up. *Do they ever come and wake you?* I get myself up.

What do you do on Saturday? We have breakfast upstairs and then we do our jobs and then I go and meet Alice. *And Sundays?*

I stay in bed on Sundays. I get up to make breakfast here and go back to bed. Sometimes I watch TV in bed.

What do you do about holidays? I haven't had any for ages – I'm saving up for it. *Do you go with your parents?* No *Would you like to have a holiday?* Yes.

What do you drink at the pub? Shandy, cider and blackcurrant. *How much does it cost?* I can't remember now.

How much does a pint of shandy cost? I can't remember – it's gone up. *How do you pay for it if you don't know?* [silence...]

If you go for a drink with Alice how do you pay for it? Alice pays for me sometimes and I pay for her sometimes. *Yes but how much money do you give them for the drink?* £3 sometimes – *and do they give you change?* Yes. *Do you get a pint of shandy for £2?* I don't know. *Do you find money difficult?*

Yes it's hard work. I used to do a lot of money at Wentwood.

When you go to get your own groceries what do you do? The staff give me the money. *How much?* £5 to buy bread – *Do they give you change?* Yes – *do you know how much change?* They give me a receipt.

How much money have you got on you? [counts out 42p correctly] *is there enough for coke?* Don't know.

When you go out for a drink… I buy a pint of shandy and Alice has a half coke – *how much is that?* I don't know – *So how much money do you go out with?* They give me my pocket money – *yes but how much do you take?* My pocket money. *So if you have a drink you won't have much left will you?*

Sometimes I get a bit more, I'm saving up for Christmas. I'm getting better on money now.

Yes but you ought to try and remember how much a drink costs shouldn't you? What do you do about money – you keep your money all week don't you?

I budget my pocket money – I get it on Mondays and Thursdays

Is that enough to buy Alice a drink when you go out?

If it isn't I get more. I've got a Post Office book and my own bank book the staff keep.

Do you get money out of the Post Office?

Yes we go ourselves. They just tell me how much I've got to write. There's a pink slip to take it out and a blue one to put the money in.

How long have you gone out with Alice? Five years, Alice's got a friendship ring and I've got a friendship ring.

Are you going to get engaged one day? I don't know yet. *You're lucky to have a girlfriend aren't you?* Yes.

Would you like to live with her one day? When the time comes, not yet.

Do you think you'd live with Alice or would you find somebody else? I'd stay with Alice.

Have your dad and mum met Alice? Yes. *Do they like her?* Yes, and I've met her family.

What do you like doing best?

I like living here with my friends – and going for a drink and having a girlfriend – I just tell them I'm going out.

If you're unhappy or you're upset and you've got a problem who do you tell? The staff. *If something goes wrong here do you tell Mum or your Dad that you're unhappy?*

Just the staff. If I'm worried I tell the staff, whoever's on duty. I like it, I'm happy here.

Sarah and David

Sarah, a 24-year-old lady with Down's syndrome, lived in a larger group home of 16 residents and emerged as the ex-student with the highest post-Wentwood score. Although increasing her life skills since leaving Wentwood, like several other very competent ladies with Down's syndrome in the sample, she appeared to find the pace of everyday life quite difficult. Her problems with cooking reflect this. She outlined the advantages and the support she gained from communal life while still retaining the privacy of her own room. At Wentwood she had had to share a room for the first and only time in her life and had disliked it intensely. It appeared that, even after much practice, she was not the most confident cook. Although a competent cook she had filled the family home up with gas two or three times, necessitating the appearance of the emergency services. She appeared to feel that the constant fire practices at her current home may also be attributable to her! Below is only part of a longer interview spread over two days. Her mother (who was also the home administrator) and siblings lived nearby in the family home.

David, aged 23, one of the least able Wentwood ex-students, also lived in the group home and had acquired a creditable 14 further skills since leaving Wentwood. He appeared to be more dependent on his parents who were separated. He expressed his emotional needs well and although his mother now lived in the village he did not want to return to live at home.

The group home was up a small wooded road, away from the main village, where the bus went to the nearby city, requiring quite a long walk whenever the residents went out. Surprisingly, they had more freedom than many residents living in urban areas and the administrator outlined below how she achieved a part of this. Much of the travel curriculum was evolved from the Wentwood model but contained a special feature to ensure every resident knew their address and phone number.

> ADMINISTRATOR: If they go into the city they usually tell us they're going because they want to, but that doesn't mean to say that we know where they are in the city.

Do they ever get lost?

> Yes. We usually say will you be back for supper. If they're not back for supper we'll keep that supper – if they're not back by 7 o'clock we might be starting to panic. If they're not back by 8 o'clock we would be starting to panic. They all know the phone number we actually taught it to all of them in a song. It was one way I taught Sarah how to speak by singing. They did a research programme at Guy's hospital with Sarah when she was young and we did it all through music – learning to speak through music. She sings everything. We had a teacher here when we first moved in and she taught them '*123456 that's the Redlands*

number' We made them sing it every morning and all the time. They all know it, so they can all actually say that number.

We have a resident here who goes off to see his parents – when he comes back he doesn't always get the right train so he ends up all over the place. He rings us up at 10 o'clock at night and says he's caught the wrong train and he's down at so and so. Someone has to go and get him. We have a procedure that the staff have to go through if a resident is lost which I have laid down and told them they must do. They've all come back! I've had contact with the police once but they've all always turned up. They all go out – some walk back from the pub in the dark – they've all got torches.

Sarah
Sarah talked about the reasons why she liked living in a group home.

Your Mum's got a house, her home, do you ever go to her home? At Christmas. *How often do you go?* Christmas.

You don't go at weekends? I don't want to – *you want to go at Christmas?* Yes I want to go at Christmas.

Why don't you want to go at other times? Well [long pause] it's fun here –

You've got friends here? Yes. *Is this your home?* Yes it is.

Is that your home where your home where your mum lives? That's where my mum lives.

It's not your home? [silence] *This is your home?* Yes my home.

Have you got any friends? Yes I have got some friends. *Have you any friends that live anywhere else?* No.

When it's your birthday do you have a party here? Yes. *Does everybody have a party?* Yes.

If you're unhappy and things wrong who do you tell? Sometimes I tell the staff – I tell the staff. *Do you tell your mum?*

Sometimes I tell my mum and sometimes I tell the staff – *who do you tell first?*

The staff. I don't like it if there's a fire alarm from burning the toast. Fire alarm goes off and you have to go outside and stand outside until it goes off

Does it happen often that the toast gets burnt? Yes.

Did you like Wentwood? I didn't really like it. *Would you rather be here?* Yes.

Why is it better here?

'Cause it's much better doing the jobs. Like getting on with it – the washing up and drying up and putting away – that's what I like doing.

You did that at Wentwood, did you learn to cook at Wentwood? Yes I learnt to cook – *would you like to go back?*

No, no thank you, I don't feel like it. I like staying here. 'Cause the staff went on a bit at Wentwood, they were always telling me what to do. I don't like the church in Wentwood. I like it here the best because it's better. I like doing things on my own. Some got a bit bossy and cross at me like telling me off.

Did you like any of the staff?

No, I like the staff here. I like it being alone in number 10, that's my room here, I've got a key to it. I like being on my own. Sometimes at the weekends I have a lie in.

Who makes the breakfast? Sometimes night staff and sometimes I make my own. *What did you have today?*

Bread and yoghurt. **I didn't make any toast** [with emphasis!]

What time do you eat at night? Normally about 6 o'clock. I've cooked but Ron's (the chef) made the cooking.

What vegetable are you having? Leeks and cabbage – *how do you cook leeks?* Like chop them. *Do you use the microwave?*

No staff only – and then put them in the bowl and then wash them – put it in the pot on the stove.

Who turns the stove on?

Staff. I'm not allowed to touch it – it's hot – I don't touch the stove thank you.

When they are cooked do staff take them off the stove? Yes. *Do you just do them when they're cold in the beginning?*

Yes. Then you put foil on and pop it in the oven keep it warm – staff put it there.

You did a lot of cooking at Wentwood didn't you? Yes. *Did you cook at home before you went?*

Yes. Sometimes when I cook it's a bit difficult on my own – it's a bit difficult on my own – I don't like cooking on my own. Like its a bit difficult. Every time I put the matches on I put it on the light and the smoke comes up and burns my hand sometimes. I put it under the cold water.

Does it sometimes go out? Yes. *So you'd rather have somebody cooking with you?*

Yes please – sometimes it makes my fingers bleed – I don't like cooking on my own I like happy cooking with Ron.

David

David talked about his emotional dependency first on his own and then with the administrator and the interviewer.

Would you rather live at Redlands or with your mum? Redlands – staff are nice. *If you're unhappy do you tell the staff?* Yes. *Are you ever unhappy?*

Yes. I go and tell staff I'm unhappy when I have any problems I go to Joan. Like I went to Henrietta when I had problems at Wentwood and she had to sort it out for me.

And did she? Yes. *What sort of problems?*

When I'm homesick and that I tell them and they tell Mum and Dad when I ask.

What's homesick? When people cry a lot. *Do you cry when you're homesick?* Yes. *Do you want your Mum?* Yes. *Do you still get homesick?* Sometimes.

What do you feel when you're homesick?

When I'm homesick – at Wentwood I had to tell Mrs McCarthy didn't I? Then she told my Mum and Dad didn't she.

And what did your Mum and Dad do? They come and get me. *How do you know when you're homesick – what do you feel?* Very angry.

Why do you feel angry?

I do a little bit but I go to the staff and they sort it out for me.

But you'd rather live at Redlands than live at home? Yes

Do you still go to your room and cry?

Yes and staff come up and they calm me down and that.

Later we were joined by staff. David's responses are in bold type.

JOAN: But you just sort of get difficult at times don't you and that's not because you are home sick is it? **No.**

What do you do to calm him down? We just talk. *He says he gets angry because he's homesick –* **yes.**

Well you've never said that before.

No only a little bit – I can give Daddy a ring sometimes don't I?

Are you homesick for Mummy or Daddy?

> **Mummy and Daddy. I always come to you when I am and then you arrange it sometimes with Daddy don't you?**

Why do you need Daddy sometimes, what for?

> **Only for a chat sometimes isn't it Joan? You leave messages sometimes when I can't get him don't you Joan?**

I do yes, sometimes his answerphone's on.

Do you talk on the answerphone? **Yes sometimes.** *What do you say?* **Daddy can you call me back?** *And does he?* **Yes.**

Sarah had been listening to the earlier part of the conversation before her mother (who was the administrator of the home and so played the dual role of mother and staff) had arrived and had been asked if she too got homesick.

Do you ever get homesick Sarah and want to go home like David? Occasionally. *What do you do?* Sometimes I cry a lot? *Do you?* Yes, sometimes I cry a lot and sometimes I hug someone.

Does that make it better if you hug someone? Yes. *Who do you hug?* Staff – *and yet you'd rather live at Redlands than live at home?* I'd rather live at Redlands, I've settled down now. *Did it take you a long time?*

> It was a bit difficult but I settled down all right. I've got a bed on my own that's why I settled down. It was too hard at Wentwood – don't want to know about it. I settled down easy at Redland – it's easier.

What makes you unhappy?

> Sometimes I cry a lot like when I'm feeling a a bit unhappy if the staff tell me off. I'm getting changed and sometimes another member of staff tells me off – what to do – and I don't like telling off.

Gareth

Gareth was an enthusiastic and likeable young man aged 26. Although not one of the most able ex-students he had matured over the past eight years within the secure environment of the group home. He had acquired a further 19 skills and was living a relatively independent life. He was currently living in the six-person training flat with two other ex-Wentwood students who came with him into the group home after leaving Wentwood. All the school leavers attended the local adult training centre who liaised with the local College of Education to enable the residents to join various part time college courses.

The spacious house and estate with garden, swimming pool youth club buildings and its own church had originally been a private children's home for many years. Some ten years ago it had changed into a private residential home for 50 children with mental handicap. Many of the children had profound multiple handicaps and there was a small special-care day unit which took young people from the home and from other areas of the city. The home had a strong religious tradition with its own church which everyone attended on Sunday afternoon. As the children grew older, where possible, they progressed up through the main home to independent living and out into the community where they were placed with local families or independent provisions. In a recent venture a house four miles away has been purchased where eight of the residents have gone to live away from the main home. One of the Wentwood ex-students chose to go but, although offered a place, Gareth chose to stay within the group home.

Eva had been at the home for 13 years and was the Group Leader of the training flat and regarded as rather more than just a member of staff by the residents. Gareth talked constantly about Eva, Eva's daughter and granddaughter and appeared to share in a little of her family life. He had borrowed Eva's video camera and had filmed both the communal life of the home and scenes of Eva's home and family.

> **I've been here since I lost my Mum. I got placed here on my seventeenth birthday here, and I had my eighteenth birthday here, and my twenty-first birthday up in the flat when I started my life, and my twenty-second birthday here**

James keeps his own money why don't you?

> **Some keep their money in their rooms. I think he's able to. It's just me and Ruth and Jill keeps theirs in the office.**

Because you're not quite sure about it?

> **That's right because Eva keeps my money – I'd rather. When I had it in my room once I found some money missing and I don't know if it was me taking it out or what. So if it's not in my room I don't take it out for things.**

When you do get your money and buy something do you know what the change is?

> **I got a problem with the change bit – what I do is give them money and get the change. We get to keep the receipt 'cause we buy our own shopping. I just bought my shopping now. I bought fruit and I bought the greengrocers stuff for us, for all six of us. On the way home after work we get our shopping. I took the money to work with me and kept it in my wallet.**

It must have been a lot of money. How much was it? **It was a pound note.**

EVA: £5 note! They all do take money and do some of the shopping on the way home and come back with the receipt and change and we check it through.

Was that enough?

Eva writes the list with us and we get it. My friends are here and the staff are my friends and I have a friend in special needs as well. I help out a lot, I help with the people there and do a lot of work with them and sit in a group with them every Wednesday morning. I chose to work with special needs to help them out.

Where do you live? **I don't live anywhere really. I live here my Nana's in D—, my Dad's in S— and this is my home now.** *Do you stay here at Christmas?* **No I go up to my Nan's and at Easter and summer sometimes.** *Have you any friends where your Nan lives?* **No all my friends are here – some have moved out now.**

What do you do for holidays? **We had a chalet at Pontins and a caravan down in Bournemouth.** *Which did you like best?* **The Bournemouth one.** *Why?*

> **It was our own caravan and we had a pub next door to it where we were and a swimming pool. When the time comes I can go on my own but I'm going with the staff for a while.**

EVA: They do have problems there. They have to face their problems as well. We had three very sad young men who spent all their money in the first two days and we had to go and get them back. We'd asked if James could go with the others on a trial because he had never been on his own so the three of them went off. And by Wednesday all their money was gone, and their food, and so was the bus fare home. They phoned up and we had to go and get them. But the next year they did manage on their own for the whole week. We usually send them when they're about to leave – if they're thinking of leaving we send them there the year before. We get them into going to to Pontins on their own so that the youngsters who have left us can go on going there on their own. We try them out before they leave here and we're in reach of them there you see. This year James went off for the first time with two young men who'd been there before they left here to live in the community with private families.

> This independence training flat was set up ten years ago with the aim of getting the youngsters who'd come through this home and were able enough to be independent. But this may change now as they rest aren't able enough to move out.

Aren't they lonely on their own? They come back and visit us like we're their family.

Gareth would you like to live on your own? **I'd like to live here but I'd like to live not on my own.** *With a family as a lodger –* **yes.** *At Wentwood you lived with a family didn't you?*

Yes when I worked at Wentwood I lived out in lodgings. You can't stay here all the time you've got to move somewhere.

EVA: Yes you can. **I'd like to stay here really I don't want to move out.** You don't have to move out no-one has ever said you have to move out.

If you want to move out you can, if not you can stay. I might want to move but till then I prefer to be staying here. We don't have staff up here like they do downstairs. We are learning to use this place for ourselves and we've got that far. All we've got the staff for like Auntie Ann and Eva is to help us do things. We do the cleaning. We've got a rota. We do our own breakfast when we want. We have to leave at 8 o'clock so if we haven't done it we go without. We do our own bedrooms and all the cleaning every six weeks on our week on. We do our own tea.

EVA: Nearly always we sit together but they might have different things.

Who gets you up in the morning?

Our alarm clocks and we get up at 7 o'clock. If we're not up somebody does make sure and they moan at us, but we're usually up before they do make sure.

I don't start moaning till 7.45 and if they haven't moved by then.

What about weekends? **You can get up when you want, we get up about lunch time when the staff come in.** *Could you stay in bed all day?* **No because you've got to get up and do things, you can't just lay around.** *Why?*

Because we won't get our jobs done and we won't be able to go out anywhere. We like to go out somewhere nice at weekends. We don't have breakfast usually – when we get up we have dinner. We all cook a proper cooked dinner. We all have a bath or shower every day. We've fruit in here and we can get food whenever we want in the kitchen.

If you're unhappy and things go wrong who do you tell?

We tell Eva any problems and if there are no staff on we save the problems up until she comes down or go downstairs and tell them?

What rules do you have here? **No rules except we can't go in bare feet because there are nails on the floor.**

Do you have keys?

> No, we did – but we all lost them. I had a key to downstairs and I lost it. Someone might lock themselves in their room without realising and when the fire bell goes we need the doors to be left open to get out easy. Boys don't go in girls' rooms or girls in boys' but each boy can go in and out of boys' rooms. We can go out on our own at night and we're all right in the dark if we're careful about it make sure there's nobody about. I like living here – I could live here for good but I want to make my own life.

Could you not make your own life here?

> I could if I wanted to but if I stay here there are more people to come and more people can't come up. If you want to live here for good and new people want to come up here, more people can't come up – because they can't share the rooms. If you want to, there isn't room.

Who said that? Did they?

> They did. This is a training place. A home for us to do training to go out with. When we finish training we move out to the community but I would really like to stay living here because I've moved out a lot. I used to move house with my parents a lot. My mum moved a lot because she was not happy. My mum lived with my dad and he walked out and married Amy and then he left Amy and went to live with Mary. Then I moved to Wentwood and then I left Wentwood and came here – and now I'd like to stay for good.

So you've moved a lot and this is the first time you've – I've settled down here *– are you happy here?* Yes. *Have you got a girl friend?* I don't want a girlfriend really *– are you thinking of getting married one day?* No. *Why?*

> Because what happened to my dad put me off marriage. This is my family home. Play me a bit of the tape 'cause I'd like to hear what we've done.

Sure – here you are, you play it back.

A problem arising in the smaller group homes run by private or larger charitable foundations (but not those with religious affiliations) was the use of residents' money. As seen, residents themselves had little understanding of the financial value of their pensions or daily needs. The excerpt below was echoed by other parents. A less serious indication is given by Bruce's mother in Chapter 2 where residents' money was used to pay for staff drinks on visits to the pub. As well as the residents it would appear that the parents are also vulnerable and hesitate to complain. The parent below was particularly strong minded and sensible with respect to her daughter's life style and did not see herself as in any way vulnerable. In almost any other situation an official enquiry would have been implemented, as her other daughter realised.

Parent

> Coming home she never had any money. The most she had was £5 and she spent £2 on her bus fare and we always gave her money for going back. This went on until I said 'I'm sure she must have more than £5 pocket money'. They were going off on holiday and she came in and said 'I'm so worried I haven't got any money for holiday'. When she left home she had £400 in her Post office book. So I rang up and said how much pocket money does she get and they said £25.25 a week. So I said she'd never had any more than £5. I said how much is in her building society book and they said 85p.

> I didn't like to make a fuss and I thought maybe they have spent the money for the holiday – you make all those sort of excuses. Anyway I had a word with my other daughter and she said I should go and inquire. I said I don't want to make a fuss – that might get one of the girls into trouble there. They would probably take it out on my daughter. You know – the mind boggles. So I rang back and said, OK she gets £25.25 and do you know what she does with it? They said they didn't know. I said she certainly doesn't bring it here and we've always had to buy her her toiletries and she's never had any clothes since she's been there. We've always bought underwear and everything. I rang again and said if she gets £25.25 I would like half of that putting in her building society book and she gets the rest. They said 'of course'. The following week she came in – would you believe it with £25.25 and also they had £80 to go into her building society book as well. So it worked. Now she puts so much in each week.

So you don't know where the money has gone?

> I'm not saying but the mind boggles. This had been going on for 12 months. I think they're vulnerable because she doesn't understand money. If you had two farthings your pocket she'd think you were very rich. She hasn't a clue. They are very vulnerable.

DISCUSSION

Although the twelve group homes visited had different philosophies, policies and training programmes, the problems of their residents were similar. The views above were repeated many times regardless of location and represent the often conflicting feelings of staff, families and residents.

There was no overall cohesive policy for group homes and each one represented the philosophy of the staff who were involved. Each had areas of excellence which could well have been emulated by others had they known about them. It became apparent that a group home is only as effective as the staff who run it. Many group homes tended to have an ever changing staff who clearly found the work stressful. In the independent sector, those group homes backed by religious foundations provided a committed and caring lifestyle with the majority of the staff having been in post for many years.

Most of the ex-students resident in group homes had family living locally yet did not wish to return to live at home. They appeared to value their work or college lives and also their relative independence. It would appear that the Wentwood philosophy of independent adult living away from the family had been well internalised and contributed to their subsequent progress and skill acquisition. Of particular interest is the fact that Redlands, with 16 residents, was the largest living unit visited. Yet the residents, like those in the smaller group homes were confident that they could express their emotional needs on an individual basis and derive comfort and support from all the staff.

Although there was no indication of any form of unified assessment system throughout the group homes, the majority of group homes had not attempted any initial assessment of any type when the resident arrived at the home. Attempts to find detailed assessments covering the years from the time each student left Wentwood to the time of the present study were destined to failure in the majority of places visited. Although many people had been in the same location for two or more years, management seemed still to be searching for a relevant assessment method. When assessing the social skills which contribute to independent living ability, the debate over methodology appears to be unhelpful. At the simplest level, either a person can do something or they cannot. Many managerial staff and key-workers were unaware that earlier Wentwood assessments indicated that students had been independent travellers, were capable of using the washing machine, cooking for themselves and competent to go shopping.

There were few signs of social skills that had already been obtained at Wentwood being recognised. Updating the final Wentwood assessments for this research at the current group homes the indication was that most ex-students had been re-taught skills they had already acquired. On request, staff were often able to provide the Wentwood assessment the student arrived with but had never referred to it as, supposedly, they used a different method. Regardless of scoring methodology, self-help skills such as washing, cooking and using public transport would seem to be self-evident and easily tested.

In the smaller homes with only two or three people living there, these very ordinary houses were still called 'group homes' by both residents and staff. Surprisingly, the various key-workers and support workers were still called 'staff' even by those independent residents, discussed in Chapter 2, whose contact with them was limited to a few hours a week and a phone number which they could call at any time. This could be interpreted as old habits dying hard but it became clear during the interviews that this terminology was continued out of choice by all the developmentally disabled people whose security and emotional support came from continuing contact with such people – rather than with their families.

The ex-students in the group homes had left Wentwood well able to live a semi-independent life and so were not fully dependent on the various training programmes in the group homes. The Wentwood curriculum had concentrated on giving each person a measure of self-sufficiency according to their ability. With hindsight, what had not been fully recognised during the two year training course was the level of emotional support that would be needed by all the students throughout their adult lives.

SALIENT ISSUES
Professionals
Assessment
Whatever method chosen, assessment of a resident's social skills should be carried out on arrival at the group home and in the environment in which the resident will be expected to live. Previous school or college records should be consulted and requested if not available. Clear records should be kept of skill gains and losses. It proved a simple task for the researcher to update the Wentwood final records even up to ten years later and equally as simple to record subsequent gains or losses.

Self Advocacy
Regardless of genuine attempts by staff in several group homes to involve the residents in empowerment and self advocacy groups it appeared that all the residents still preferred the staff to make policy decisions.

In the light of the continuing emotional dependence of residents it could be helpful if residential staff and key-workers ran self advocacy classes within the group homes. Such work would then be meaningful to the residents who would become aware that they could work through their own staff to implement changes. When outsiders ran such classes the ex-students appeared to find difficulties in generalising the concepts back to their own lives. The example of Lily's inability to ask to go riding occurred in many forms throughout the interviews. Had Ann been running the class for Tom and his friends it was unlikely that they would have gone to sleep or refused to join in.

Electrical Gardening Tools
The relatively simple action of providing a circuit breaker for the lawn mower was only found in the one group home. The smaller homes in Chapter 2 also also had no such provisions. Wentwood had trained everybody to look after a garden and although several ex-students clearly remembered and enjoyed

this activity, it was usually regarded as too difficult to arrange for them to continue to do so in the group home. Several were clearly disappointed.

Parents
Finance
If parents are concerned about the financial arrangements implemented by the staff in a group home they should ask for a clear, preferably written, statement of financial policy. Although it must be emphasised that their children are now young adults learning to gain increased control over their financial dealings, the evidence presented in this research is that residents have imperfect understanding of their finances. They rely, even when living independently, almost completely on staff and key-workers to help them budget their money.

Several parents expressed similar concerns to those shown by the parent, who was anxious to remain anonymous, about aspects of financial management in group homes. Conversely, several managers of independent group homes expressed equal concern about the lack of money available for residents' holidays and personal use. The interview with the manager of Jane and Allan's group home was repeated many times and it appeared that some parents assumed that now their child was 'in care' financial aspects were no longer their concern, except for birthday and Christmas presents.

Parents could inquire if extra finances would be helpful. Many years ago MENCAP and other charitable organisations raised their initial funding from jumble sales and coffee mornings. Several older parents who remembered those days expressed a wish to continue such activities. The researcher, when running unit for MENCAP parents, was well aware of the pleasure parents found in taking an active interest in fund raising. It may well be that group homes would would welcome such an approach and have their own suggestions of how parents could help.

Independence
The problem of parental contact was difficult for several residents. They were happy and well settled in their group homes and often wished to join in communal activities or spend time with a special friend rather than go home to visit parents. These same residents also confessed to being homesick sometimes as can been seen in the interviews! Possibly it would be helpful if the family consulted group home staff as to the best course to take at any particular time, especially at Christmas. Parents will almost certainly have experienced similar problems with their other adult offspring.

CHAPTER 2

Home

THE FAMILY HOME

The 30 per cent of ex-students who still remained in the family home were in the least advantageous circumstances and overall had lost substantially more skills than the people living in group homes or independently. As a group, their Wentwood final assessment scores were of a similar distribution to the other two groups and their home surroundings contained many more material benefits and potential learning opportunities than was to be found the living environments of the other two groups.

In the majority of cases the type of living unit did not appear to interfere with the available options of work, work-experience, college or adult centre. The occupational status of the people living at home was similar to that of other ex-students but there was some indication that for their families the adult centre was an easier and preferred option for ladies living at home.

There was a preponderance of single parent families in the home group and also of ex-students who wanted no contact with their similarly disabled peers. Sadly, the main interest of aging parents was the comfort and well being of their offspring. It was tragic to see grown men and women being cosseted by such devoted parents. They were bathed, dressed, fed and cared for like small children. Even some ex-students travelling independently to work during the day returned home at night to such cosseting. For many a lonely parent the wellbeing of their son or daughter gave some focus to their lives.

Trevor

The following life style was typical of many; a mother over-protected her 20-year-old son to a such an extent that she would not leave him alone in the house in case he touched the hot cooker even though his full time job was in the kitchens of a large canteen! Both parents did everything for their son and wherever they went – he went. They had refused an invitation to a New Year's Eve party because he wouldn't go and they felt unable to leave him in the house alone or get a sitter to keep an eye on him. Trevor had gained 21 skills since leaving Wentwood, mainly through having stimulating and interesting work. He had also lost nine far more important self-help skills of the type needed for successful semi-independent living in a group home. He lived a reclusive life and never left the family home except to go to work or out with his parents.

Mother's interview

What happens if you're not in when Trevor comes in from work? I'm always in.

Does he do any cooking here or make his breakfast?

We prepare it for him. My husband gets it ready when he gets up at 4 am for work. Trevor gets up with me. We get up together – I get up at 6 o'clock because I've got a little job. Trevor leaves at 7 o'clock and I leave at 7.20.

What time do you get up in the morning Trevor? **6 o'clock.**

What time do you go to bed at night? **10 o'clock.**

That's early; do you go because you're tired? **No.**

I draw the curtains for him about 10 – he don't get to bed till about quarter to eleven.

So you send him to bed at ten every night do you? Yes, yes,

What about weekends?

No we all get up later at weekends. He likes to have a lay in on Saturday and Sunday.

Other families rationalised the decision to keep their children at home and went to great lengths to ensure they can continue to work when they hold good jobs. Often their children admit to being lonely at home and, having lost many self-help skills, are now no longer capable of sustaining any sort of semi-independent life-style.

Julie

Julie, aged 24, who does complex work in an electronics firm, has gained no skills since leaving Wentwood and lost 20 valuable self-help life skills.

MUM: We worry about what will happen to Julie. We wanted her home. This friend of hers, she's gone into a flat on her own but she's more able than Julie in lots of ways – but Dad was saying, really if you think about it it's not terribly nice living on your own – he feels it would be better if she was sharing with somebody. I went away for a month and he came back after a fortnight and he said that the fortnight that I was away – it was lonely coming home every night to an empty house – even for a fortnight – I don't think Julie will ever be able to cope on her own like that.

Amanda

Amanda was a tall, attractive well dressed 22-year-old. She was shy, with a tendency to get bored, but very polite, Since leaving Wentwood two years ago she was now doing two college courses on different sites and travelling by two buses each morning from her rural farmhouse home. She walked through the town from one college to another each day. Her parents usually gave her a lift to the 8'clock bus every morning as transport was difficult if she missed it. Amanda was passionate about cards and could beat her grandmother and often her father. She played whist, patience and rummy yet proved quite unable to handle money!

Amanda was an average Wentwood student and although shy was well liked and made steady, though not spectacular, progress. Since returning home she had lost only two skills and increased her final Wentwood assessment by five skills and managed to live a full and relatively independent life. She was unusual in that her parents allowed her to handle all the money that was due to her and only sorted it out after she had drawn her allowance from the Post Office. Her interview indicated she was happy with her life and well in control but she was very shy and did not volunteer information easily. So much so, that her answer to the final question came as rather a surprise.

Mother

What did Wentwood do for Amanda?

She hated leaving home she'd never left before –

(A: I was crying my eyes out.)

She hated it at first and when we took her sisters to visit her after three weeks the girls came back and were very upset. They said it wasn't fair to send her. But then most of the time she loved it. I think they gave her independence. I couldn't believe the things she did. Really we'd have been frightened at home to let her do these things. She used to catch the train home and back in the holidays.

She handles all the money that's due to her?

She handles it by putting it all into her bedroom and every so often we say we've got to go along to the building society and put some money in. She pays for her hair and clothes etc. You have an awful job to get her to spend money – she's not very good at spending money.

Does she spend your money? If she's not spending her own is she spending yours?
No she spends her own.

Amanda

Is there anything that you want to do that you can't do? I can't do money. *Do you want to do money?* Yes. *Does that bother you that you can't do money?* Yes.

Why? Because I can't give money to people – like shop people. *Does that bother you?* Yes. *You'd like to be able to do that would you?* Yes. *What else bothers you?* Just money. *Do they teach you money at college?* Yes *Do you find it difficult there?* Yes *Which bits of money?* I can't give it to shopkeepers. *Does that make you unhappy?* Yes – *but you go to the village shop with money don't you?* Yes. *What about the change?* The shopkeeper gives the change to me. I can't do the money bit. *The only thing that bothers you is money – is everything else all right?* Yes.

Ada

Ada, aged 28, leads a reasonably independent life. Although partially sighted, she is left at home on her own when she is not working. This has enabled her to have an overall skill gain and only one skill loss. Her mother described some of her own ambivalences.

Mother

What do you reckon that Wentwood did that you couldn't do?

> I think they made her more independent. When she went out on her own catching the bus – I wouldn't have let her do that.

Would you ever have let her?

> I don't know. I suppose I would have in the end – I don't know. It's difficult – at one time she did want to go and live in a house on her own – from Wentwood – I didn't want her to but we did put her name down but she didn't get it.

Why not? They said she wasn't quite suitable. *Would you want her to share a house?* Not particularly but if she wants to do it – but I don't think she'd cope.

What's going to happen to her when you get very old?

> I don't know. This is why she's been to all these different places hoping she could cope on her own. I'm hoping the other children will be there for her.

You mean she'd have to live with them?

> If something didn't crop up and she didn't live on her own – yes. She gets lonely on her own.

Nick

Nick, aged 25, had no wish to leave home and was quite content with his life. He had lost 18 important self-help skills whilst gaining only six lesser ones due to his gardening work. His mother was happy to look after him and he was content to live at home, as shown in the three way conversation below. Nick left Wentwood well able to cope with semi-independent living. Although he copes well with his gardening work it is unlikely that he would now be able to be self-sufficient.

MUM: When they opened this hostel they offered him at a place at it. *How far away is it?* Just down the road – *so he could have walked home every night?*

Oh yes – but that's not really the point if he's meant to be independent. But they get so much hassle from the others it wouldn't be worth it.

Do you want to leave home Nick? **No way!** *Why not?* **I don't want to leave my family and my friends.**

What about all this independence they talk about? Living on your own and being independent, you don't want to do that? **No!**

What if you lived just next door but one. You could still see your friends?

No it means I wouldn't be able to see Mum as much. I live here every day –

And you like that do you? **Oh yes.**

If you could live at home with Mum and do all things you did at Wentwood would you rather do that or work where you are now?

I'd rather do the things I done at Wentwood.

Can you cook, if mum were ill could you cook something? **I could.**

Can he cook?

He used to cook at Wentwood but he doesn't cook here – he makes toast – he makes his own breakfast.

So mum does all the cooking?

That's right – and all the washing and all the ironing. He's supposed to clean his room... He cleans his room yes – he shoves all his clothes in the cupboard.

You don't actually want him to go and live away do you?

Oh no, I believe in looking after my own – anyway he's no trouble really – a lot of laughs and no trouble.

Sandra

Sandra, aged 28, is of particular interest as she went to Wentwood with Tom and John and all three families lived in the same suburb within a mile of each other – as is the hostel that Tom and John are in now. Sandra reads well, uses a computer to write her letters and has an overwhelming interest in classical music. Her speech is good and she has excellent communication skills. She was the only person to ask the interviewer sensible questions and initiate a conversation around her musical interests, getting her library book to illustrate difficult points. Her recorded IQ is between 35 and 40. Divorced, with one other sibling still at home, her mother works part time in one of the caring professions.

Sandra goes to the adult centre every day and to the MENCAP club each week where she still sees Tom and John. Having completed the same two year training course at Wentwood with them and returned to the same suburb with its attendant public facilities her life is now very different. Since leaving Wentwood ten years ago she has not left the house on her own. She spends two weeks every year in respite care where she is said to settle down very quickly. The rest of her life is lived with her mother who takes her anywhere she wants to go such as concerts and museums. She has relatives and is included in their parties with her mother. The interview, like so many, emphasised the fact that very few of the ex-students had been able to communicate to their families their enjoyment of work and independence whilst at Wentwood. For people who returned to live in the family home, Wentwood seemed to have been a quite separate environment and they were unable to continue with, and generalise, the skills they had been taught because of the lack of practice. The family home was in a neighbourhood with many potential facilities of which Sandra had few opportunities to avail herself.

Excerpts from the final Wentwood assessments are particularly relevant to Sandra's subsequent lifestyle.

BEST POINTS
Friendly and cheerful. Language clear when interested. Understands environment and changing circumstances. Interested in current affairs, outings, concerts and all social occasions. reads notices, takes action and remembers.

WEAK POINTS
When with others road safety non-existent. Nevertheless does go about town alone, does errands and returns safely.

Sandra's interview

What did you do at Wentwood? **Looked after children in a nursery, they were always good.** *What did you do with them?* **Played.** *How did you get there?* **By bus.** *By yourself?* **Yes.**

If there was a nursery here would you like to work there? **Yes.**

Why don't you ask at the centre? **They don't do it. You know the lollipop people that help children cross the road?** *Yes, would you like to do that?* **Yes.**

Do you like children? **Yes.** *Have you got any children in the family?* **No.** *Was that the best thing about Wentwood – the children?* **Yes, and we went to concerts in Bath and Bristol.**

Mother comes in to join the conversation.

Sandra said she enjoyed her work experience job with the children in Wentwood?

Did you Sandra? What did you do with the children? How fascinating, I knew she worked at the hairdresser but not a nursery. Are you sure it wasn't a plant nursery Sandra?

No children. She never told me.

If Mummy were to find you a playgroup to go to would you like that? **Yes.**

It was called structured leisure at Wentwood which I think was extremely good but they did organise it all. It'll be like everything else – you have to jog her along. Sandra doesn't want to work – they've tried her from the centre at an old people's home. She can do the work – she can polish but she doesn't want to – she just wants to listen to her music. If she didn't want to go to an old people's home and dust all the tops and wash all the basins I didn't see why she should. I know some children get a lot of pleasure from those sort of things. They get pleasure from it and they like to be praised for it but Sandra hasn't got that nature. She doesn't want to work.

When she came out of Wentwood I didn't want her to go to a hostel because I didn't think much of them – they may have improved now but at the time there was a lot I didn't like about them. She would survive on a desert island – she's a loner – she hasn't any friends even at the club she goes to. She doesn't want to live away in a hostel. I thought about it one time but at that time there were one or two things happening about the town – and I just felt I didn't want her to go to one of those places.

I wanted her to stay at Wentwood longer but they couldn't keep her longer – they couldn't do any more for her. Sandra used to be put on the train from Wentwood and I used to meet them all off the train at the station. When they went back to Wentwood I used to get a taxi and pick all four of them up and put them on the train and they used to get out at Melksham.

How do you see her future?

I just don't know. I don't think about it too much. She'll go to respite care for a fortnight each year but she's not happy about it. I think anywhere you go – any urban area they're extremely vulnerable.

Why? I just think they are.

Shirley

Shirley, a very large 24-year-old lady with Down's syndrome, lived with her mother and came from a closely knit church-going West Indian family. The three children had been born in Jamaica and were looked after by their grandmother until Shirley, the youngest was eight, by which time their mother was settled in a good job in England. The grandmother then brought the children to join their mother and looked after them while she worked. History repeated itself and Shirley's mother, now retired from nursing, looks after her daughter's child. One daughter, interviewed before her mother arrived home, had very clear ideas about Shirley's place in the family. The other sister, a single parent, went to a great deal of trouble to contact the interviewer at a later date to talk about Shirley.

Shirley was one of the least able Wentwood ex-students and on her return home had, within a year, lost 21 skills. The interviewer had lunch with Shirley at Wentwood where she was living in the independent house, and watched her cook the meal. Sitting next to her during lunch she had noted her good social skills and had a reasonable conversation with her. Records indicate that she was not particularly happy at Wentwood but point out that on holidays in the caravan with staff 'she can be one of the busiest, sensible most helpful people. She cooked, cleaned, washed up to the point where she had to be told to go and sit down.' They also note that in routine matters she was lazy. In lessons 'it was like getting blood out of a stone'. Records also indicate that Shirley's self-help skills were somewhat complicated because on top of the Wentwood hygiene regime, she had to follow 'a complicated routine of grease on her hair, lotion on body, vaseline on face etc.' The etc. is not specified but it was noted that she did all these things without prompting at home but did not always remember at Wentwood.

It was clear that however much lip-service was paid to independent living it was unlikely that the West Indian culture would welcome such a move. Shirley is included in the study to indicate that in some cultures the current mode of educating people with learning disabilities towards fully independent living may not be truly appropriate. Shirley had little to say about her life but seemed happy within the family home and able to look after herself.

Shirley's sister

Josephine was an attractive and highly articulate student at a nearby college. She described how the family social life revolved round church, which Shirley enjoyed.

> The Pentecostal Church is a family-orientated church. There are so many families in church that it's not only for worship but we tend to mainly see our relatives in church. West Indians are very God orientated not only in going to church but a real belief in God from an early age. It's to do with your own personal commitment and 80 per cent are young people at our particular church.

Was Mum happy about Shirley going to Wentwood?

Mum kept saying she won't be back until 1990 and obviously the psychological fact of 90 sounds like forever. In that sense she wasn't happy about her going. She likes her at home best.

What will Mum do when she gets really old?

Well she was planning to sort something out but I said we'd have to talk about that some more anyway, because if she's not here – we'll be around.

Who is we? We as in my sister and myself. *Do you want her for the rest of your life?*

I don't mind, she's my sister and I'm quite prepared to have her stay with me. Really I'd prefer to know that she's with me than being away. Actually, to be honest I think for the main my sister would want her to stay too. I wouldn't want her to go away.

But it's a terrific thing to take on for the whole of your life.

It's not being that generous really because she's my sister. Especially if I was in the position to have her, I don't see why not really. Also it leaves the resources for someone who doesn't have any family.

You really would take on Shirley for the rest of your life? I would honestly. *Even if you had children of your own?* Yes I would because it's not any extra problem because she is independent anyway. *Well she doesn't go out on her own –*

Well I'm hoping it will change now I'm back. I'm hoping that Mummy will, for her sake. I've always been saying she should but I've not been here to persuade my Mum to see that she needs to do that. I love my sister and I'd rather know that she's with me. It's the family. It's better to keep the family together than have to be away with other people.

What happens if you get married or live with somebody and your fellow doesn't want her? I would hope that the person I would choose would be understanding of that really. *Has your mother asked you to take her?* No. *Does she assume you will?*

No she doesn't. She plans for her to stay in a long stay place locally but she hasn't really mentioned it in detail to us. We'll have to see what Shirley wants herself, obviously. She would be able to make that kind of decision.

If your mother was ill could Shirley look after her?

Yes, she could make her a cup of tea and some food. I'm sure she could do most things but it's just that my Mum is very protective.

Mother

> *What does she do at college?*

What they teach her at college is what she's done before – just reading and writing. We just can't get her to do any reading or things like that – you see she's not interested in things like that. Somebody takes her swimming but I don't know if it's a volunteer or what.

Is it a key worker? I don't know. *Does she have a key worker?* I don't know who it is.

> *She doesn't go on the bus on her own?*

No, that's a problem with my daughter. She says I cloak her too much. You know, she says I should let her but it's a bit complicated you see. It's not a straightforward journey. She's no problem at all. The only trouble, but it's not a problem really, is if I'm going out to the shops I don't leave her on her own.

Why not? Well if you said 'Shirley if anybody comes to the door' – she will open it you see. *Have you a chain on the door?* No it won't fit a glass door.

> *How do you see her future – what would you like for Shirley?*

I don't know, the social worker was talking, they intend to build some houses. I don't know how long it will be to do some here. She could live four in a house with somebody just to look over them.

But she would have to learn to go out on her own – yes – I know [laughs]

What's your main problem with her? I can't think of any really – she looks after my granddaughter.

Tara

Tara, aged 20, lives with her father who exerts what could be seen as an undue amount of control over her life. Tara's life is merely a more extreme version of the life style of many of the ex-students who lived in the family home. Due to parental intervention several of the females had also had menstruation stopped by various means. In every case there was clear evidence in the Wentwood records that they had been taught how to cope with their periods and if they had arrived at Wentwood without such expertise, they had left coping well.

Tara was a charming articulate young lady who could read and write well. She had remarkably good conversational skills although not being one of the most able students at Wentwood. Since living at home for two years she had lost seven life skills and would lose many more due to lack of practice. Her father cared about her progress and in a recent attempt to help her tell the time had bought her an effective talking clock. He was present throughout most of the interview and her responses are in bold type.

Apart from attending college and going over to a neighbour for an hour or two at night Tara's time is spent with Daddy who is reluctant to allow her out of his sight. Daddy takes her to buy clothes, on holiday, does all the washing, cleaning and cooking. Tara is responsible for her own money, pays her rent and gets her own pension from the Post Office. She also is able to travel independently on the bus to college in a large town.

Do you go shopping by yourself on the way home?

No, I'm not allowed. Daddy won't allow me to go by myself in town but I get milk for Daddy round here. I get my allowance from the Post Office and then I come straight home and we sort it out between us.

How do you sort it out?

Daddy has half for my keep and washing and what he does tomorrow and I keep the rest myself. I've got my bank account and Post Office book. Daddy gets the shopping and I help him – I keep him in order. We go Friday – and sometimes we go for coffee or tea after.

Who's going to come for your 21st party?

Daddy's organising it for me aren't you Daddy and inviting every one. His friends from work – aren't you Daddy? About a dozen are coming.

DAD: I do all the cooking.

Do you cook at college? **Yes.** *Have you got a microwave?* **Yes** *– you could use that here.* **Daddy says it's too difficult, isn't it daddy?** Yes it's too complicated for her.

Daddy's busy on a Sunday doing the washing and by the time he's done that it's time for dinner – and you've got to do the floor haven't you after that?

Why don't you do the floor? She'll get more water on the floor than in the bucket. **Daddy does it, he's cleverer than me.** *You're quite a clever young lady sorting all your money out like you do.*

If you're unhappy and things go wrong at college – who do you tell? **Daddy, every Monday!**

She went backwards since she left Wentwood – but she's done more this last year at college than she did in the last two years. When you go down to open days they just fob you off when you ask why she's gone back.

Do you understand money at all? **No – a little bit – not a lot.** *If you go and buy something what do you do?*

> **Give them a pound and get change back but I don't buy any Coke any more because I've got to lose weight haven't I Dad?**

How much was Coke? **I can't remember. I buy the milk for Daddy.** *How much do you pay?* **65.** *Do you try and give them the right money?* **No a pound.**

Who does all your washing? **Daddy.** *Do you do any of your own washing by hand?* No I do it all on a Sunday. *Who does the ironing?* **Daddy, he's fussy with his shirts** – *but you did iron at Wentwood?* **Yes but he's fussy.**

(Tara worked at an old people's home a day a week, organised by college, and had a work book to show what she did. She wrote this up herself with no difficulty. It appeared to be full of making tea, washing up and cooking. She noted each resident who died, which upset her. Each day finished with glowing reports of her work written by the staff.)

Do you ever do the vegetables here? **No there's not a potato left when she's finished.** *Is there anything you don't like doing there?*

> **I like all of it – I'd like to work there. I cleaned and polished all the furniture. I chopped and cooked the carrots for dinner.**

Do you do all the cleaning and polishing here? **No.** *Why not, then Daddy wouldn't have to do it. You do make him work hard. Couldn't she help you a little bit?*

> **Daddy likes it quiet on a Sunday and he likes to get on with the washing and he doesn't want me on at him all time – do you?**

> She used to peg the clothes out but they were all over the place. The home care lady comes on a Friday 4–6 after she comes back from college and takes her out shopping – and I go as well.

What's the home care lady? Someone to take her out – *is this the key worker?* No she looks after people like Tara. *Does she take you both in the car?* Yes. We used to go shopping on a Saturday and get a taxi back with the bags.

I must go home now – **but I haven't finished talking yet** – *so you keep saying and I'm sitting quietly waiting for you to finish writing and talking. Hurry up I want to go home now. I'll write to you and you can write back to me.*

> **I don't have periods any more – Daddy didn't like them – he had them stopped – by injections.**

> Yes – I couldn't cope with the mess – there was blood all over the floor.

Bruce

Bruce was the least able ex-Wentwood student with virtually no communication skills which made it particularly difficult for his parents. He was a good looking ginger haired 28-year-old with Down's syndrome. Since living at home he had lost 11 of the few skills recorded at his final Wentwood assessment. As he was unable to communicate the interview took place with his mother and Bruce eventually retreated upstairs. He lived in a very beautiful residential area with large houses with gardens and swimming pools backing onto woods. It was however, poorly served for little corner shops, public transport, pubs and other helpful aids to independence. He attended the local adult centre while his parents tried to find somewhere that will offer a permanent home for him as they are nearing retirement age.

His mother devoted most of her time to him and although he is 28 still regarded him as a child. Nevertheless, however overprotective she may appear, many of the individual points she made were echoed by other parents who were equally as protective of their adult 'children'. The MacIntyre organisation that she decried had been recognized by most parents and several ex-students as the one that most fulfilled all their needs. In Chapter 2 Angela saw it as the place she would most like to live, as did Gillian and her mother in Chapter 5.

There were also many parents who were concerned about the use or abuse of their children's financial assets as seen in other chapters. Bruce's mother mirrored the feelings of many parents who had worked for organisations like MENCAP in the days when people were struggling to better the conditions of their mentally handicapped children.

Mother

He's doing now what he did when he left Wentwood. We knew that if he didn't have the motivation and stimulation that he had at Wentwood he would go down, which he has done. He has not kept up with the routines and things that he had when he left.

The taxi comes for him at eight and I think it's a long day for a boy who is not sometimes very well – and therefore sometimes I don't send him in during the week because he looks so exhausted – not because he's really ill. I just think 'all right I can turf you out of here and want rid of you' but I can't do that.

He can dress himself but Mummy usually tidies him up and tucks the shirt in. If he's slow during the week I do give him a hand when the taxi is coming but at the weekend he dresses himself. He has a bath every night. I check the water and this is where my sister thinks I spoil him. I wash his back and she said to me 'who washes your back?' He dries himself after a fashion. He has an electric razor and I think he could do it but father is meticulous – he's from a military family!

What do you do about holidays with him? We have to take him on holiday with us – *you don't put him in respite care?*

> That's no holiday for him. We go to a cottage which is a change of air but not exactly a holiday for us because he will be with us. He needs a change too.

Does he go to church?

> No, I do go to church, and I could take him, but by the time I've got him ready it's a bit too long. At the weekend we don't rush out as we do during the week. He goes at Christmas and Easter. I go every week myself. He didn't take communion because he wouldn't understand it and they are meant to understand about communion aren't they? On the other hand he's gone up with me and the priest puts his hand on his head. He might not even like the wine and that's the problem. It might be so awful if he spat it out. That is the thing.

Do you ever think about respite care?

> I might but I do think it's one sided and he needs a change too. You're between two stools. I think 'putting him in there that's dead easy... let's go on our own for a week and have a lovely time...' but he needs to go too. I would take him by myself on a holiday but I would like someone to come with me. It would be too hard by myself. We have taken him to a house in Majorca with a swimming pool. It was a bit hot and he spent most of the day in the swimming pool.
>
> He doesn't have much of a social life – I used to send him to Gateway but they did nothing for him. He once went when he was much younger and I was telling the helper that he couldn't communicate very well. The head came over and said in front of everybody that I was a fussy mother. I was very emotional about that and never sent him again. I am a fussy mother, yes. He gets easily infected in these crowded rooms and these children aren't very strong.

You and your husband give all your leisure time to Bruce?

> I get a helper to see to Bruce on Monday and my husband and I go out once a month to play bridge and we get a sitter. I think my husband sometimes resents that we don't have more time together. I was a nurse and a midwife but I didn't work because of Bruce.
>
> You know every child like Bruce would like to be at home, let's be honest, but that can't happen. They'd rather live at home but that isn't practical when parents are getting on and I've always thought it's our problem not my children's problem because no one looks after a child as well as his mother does – you can't expect that sort of care elsewhere I know that. My husband is due to retire and I think that possibly I

should be giving him a bit more time. We're both devoted to Bruce but I feel that maybe its time to. He went to a local authority hostel about three years ago. I think he lasted three to four months.

When you went to see him was he upset or were you upset?

We were rather upset at the way they handled Bruce when we were on holiday. They moved him out of his room while we were away and didn't tell us. They put him down in a grotty room near the kitchen and didn't tell us. He'd been right beside a bathroom before and they decided that they would make his bedroom into a sitting room for staff or whatever. I was never truly happy about him going to a training centre when he was there. They never took them out to local facilities – and if they did it was a pub. These youngsters pay for their helpers to have drinks and they had no transport and they didn't use the lovely leisure centre. He goes there now with the epileptic colony, we take him every weekend.

Did he look happy when you went to see him?

It's difficult to tell, I used to take him home every weekend. My husband is very keen that we send Bruce to a place but I have reservations about the training centre. I know he can be happy. He needs to be away from us, we're old – providing he can get the right sort of care. He needs quite a lot of care in the sense that he needs the emotional and loving care, plus the young life of a young man. One has to look at his health a little bit. Wentwood got the best out of him.

I went to the MacIntyre home where I was horrified – they had these lovely chalets in the grounds and they had a huge old building with big rooms and one lady took us round. One of the Down's was in a sort of pink combination suit and unshaven. We went to these chalets where they were going to have a meal soon and there was girl smoking a fag and no sign of a meal. The youngsters had gone to get it – apparently they have a lot from Marks and Spencer. One of the young handicapped people followed us with no shoes or socks on and one of the helpers said 'Oh, she likes to walk like that' and it was a cold frosty autumn day. You've only got to do that for mother to get the wrong idea.

What did you want for Bruce, what did you want from Wentwood?

I hoped that Bruce would get the stimulation and would further his education. I think he did, but it would have to have been kept up. He went right down when he left. What do you do with someone like Bruce who is not all that able. Bruce's future is my one aim now.

Can you clarify in your own mind what you want for Bruce?

I would like something that is not too far away, an hour or an hour and a half at the most, so I can come and pick Bruce up once a month or once a fortnight. I would like him to have younger friends and be more motivated. A couple of young lads he can kick a football with – a room to himself.

I saw what social services didn't do for his social life. They had him sitting there and the pub was the only thing they did and they had the leisure centre right there – and they paid for staff drinks. They had no transport. The manager never came to the meetings nor did the social worker. I thought the kitchen was old fashioned and totally inadequate for the numbers they cooked for. An old cooker and an old kitchen for 12 residents and there again they sent out for take-away food because nobody was wanting to cook.

There's all this business of choices that we don't entirely agree with. If you smile at him and say 'Bruce you like this don't you?' He'll say 'yes'. If Bruce is well cared for and loved – of course no-one can love him like we do – and looked and seemed happy in that routine, I would be happy for him. Of course no-one can love him like we do.

Bruce is a big boy now. Of course that's the wrong attitude, he's a young man and we don't treat him as a young man. I was never the greatest of person to have a Down's. I could love him but I can't give that time to sit down and teach him. I haven't done that and you have to do that. I prefer to look after him in a caring way as long as he's happy but I'm not sure I like being tough with him.

INDEPENDENT LIVING

There were so many different types of independent living provisions visited that it is difficult to categorise them. However, two placements were particularly disturbing. The first, in supported lodgings was established well before the advent of the Care in the Community Act and had been used by a particular local authority for some years. All the people concerned in the placement described below were uneasy about the adequacy of such provisions for people with developmental disabilities. The interview was attended by both parents, the ex-student and the member of staff now in charge of his current group home placement. They speak for themselves.

Andrew

Andrew was a good looking, well dressed, 28-year-old man with dark curly hair and, due to his current girlfriend's influence, a recently pierced ear. He spoke well and wittily. Devoted to his mountain bike he rode all over the local area, which was provident as his current recent placement was in a disused mental subnormality hospital so totally isolated that its whereabouts was not even known by local people. The institution was being run down and there were only two people in his wing but he was very happy there. Andrew's increased skill level of a creditable 20 skills had almost certainly been acquired through the need to cope with adversity.

Parents

> He went to Wentwood and then he came home and lived with us. Then he went to the training centre and while he was there, going from home, this supported lodgings scheme came up which was run by the district council. While he was there the wife took up teaching and couldn't go on with the lodgings so another supported lodgings was found for him and he was there for three years up to this time last year. Then he came here. While he was at the last supported lodgings he had several bouts of depression – things just got on top of him.

Because you didn't like it Andrew? **Yes I ran away.**

When you ran away where did you go? **Anywhere.** *Did you sleep out at nights?* **Yes I did.** *Whereabouts?* **In the town.** *Were other people sleeping out?* **No.** *Did anybody move you on?* **No.** *The police didn't find you?* **Eventually.** *Did you try and hide from the police?* **I was asleep.**

Parents

> He just took off on his bike – the first time he ever done it he was at home. It always seems to be associated with the opposite sex. With girls I'm afraid. It has happened now five or six times. We don't know why he gets on his bike and just goes. He doesn't know where he's going or for what reason. The first time he was found by my friend in the next village and she rang us up and sent him back and he came back as if nothing had happened. This time last year he had a massive break-in to a girl's house and did some damage to the door and was making a general nuisance of himself – I don't think he realised what he was doing he was so away. They got the police and he finished up at the police station and they got in touch with his landlady. She came and got him out, after a lot of persuasion, as he'd done damage to somebody's property. She explained what happened. From then he gradually got worse and worse in the end she couldn't cope with him and called the GP in and he admitted him to hospital. He was there from December to February and he was in a bit of a state.

Andrew are you happier living somewhere where there's staff? **Yes.** *You like it with staff?* **Yes.**

Staff member

They're often lonely on their own. This is a big old building and they've got a lot of space here. They've got company if they want it and, if they want, they've also got the space that they can take themselves off somewhere away.

Parents

Another problem with this supported lodgings is – its a good thing in a way – but then the landlady that is charge of the person lodging there – they have their own family and it's not the same as when you've got staff. When you've got staff they are there to look after you. Although staff have their own family, I know – but they are paid to do that looking after.

Staff

That's right – but supported lodgings are supposed to be run so that when someone goes in to a family they become part of the family – but it doesn't work.

Is that what they are supposed to be? Yes, they're supposed to be part of the family – *that I didn't know –*

And they've been kept in their bedrooms and they're not allowed to go into the other rooms. The family also gets a lot of money.

Parents

This time last year he would never ever have got into that state if he had been in a place like Wentwood or if he'd have been living at home. He'd have never got into that state or gone to that extreme. It's to get attention. I don't really know what it is but it would never have happened if he'd been in a place like this. They all work together – the doctor, the psychiatric nurse, the community nurse so they can monitor his medication and behaviour. With regard to us it's nice to know that somebody else is watching.

The other placement was more disturbing as it was a direct result of the increased funding available in the wake of the new enthusiasm for care in the community. As such, it may well become the sort of provision to be replicated in other geographical areas. It was difficult to establish the intention of the local authority regarding this placement which they had approved and found at the request of the parents. Presumably it was a hybrid developed from an imperfect understanding of either supported lodgings or semi-independent living provision in the community.

Leslie

Leslie was a rather difficult 22-year-old who was living with two other people in a large semi-detached house in a newly established venture. The unit consisted of two adjacent semi-detached houses with the three residents having one house to themselves and a family of husband and wife and their four young children aged eight, six, five, and three years old living in the other. The houses were totally separate with two adjacent front doors but no further connection. The management of the residents was idiosyncratic and left no scope for further development of self help or personal life skills. The residents' house was adequately furnished but the atmosphere was barren. Although they had a perfectly adequate kitchen there was no food in the house and the residents, regardless of the weather, took their plates to the other house to get food at mealtimes. They carried them down both garden paths out into the street to eat back in their own house. When finished they took the plate back to be washed up. There was no attempt to make the meal a social experience by setting a table and sitting down together. The residents were expected to have their main meal at college or the adult centre and were usually just given a snack at night. The phone was permanently switched through to the other house and they went out to use the public phone box in the street.

The residents were included in family outings and the father often took Leslie off to play golf. Leslie often went with the family when they all cycled to town. He travelled independently to his college course and was competent to go out on his own using public transport. The area, on the outskirts of the town, was well served by public transport and shops. Leslie went home for a weekend once a month and didn't appear to cause any problems there. He was at the family home during the interview with his parents and looked happier and more relaxed than in his own home. Leslie was not one of the more able Wentwood students and although he had only been in the placement for six months he had already lost three self-help skills and would certainly lose many more in the future due to lack of opportunity or practice. He was the only person in this group with an overall skill loss. The conversation below, as are all quotations throughout, was taken directly from the transcription with the house manager and parents.

House manager

> I've never seen any records but was just told things by the social worker. I just don't believe he did all those things at Wentwood. I don't believe any of it. Leslie can't even have a conversation with anybody so how could he have gone about on his own? We have lots and lots of problems with information passed on and I don't know if people try to give you all the best things and hope that you're going to believe them but they're a load of rubbish. I don't know where they get their

information from. The social workers do the assessment so I don't really see them, but now they're living with me they don't have a social worker.

Do they have a key worker? No, just me.

I do the cooking and we all eat the same meal but they eat in their house and we eat next door. They carry it through. They bring their plates in to me and I give them their dinner on a tray. We don't always have pudding as they prefer to eat their cooked dinner at lunch time and have snacks in the evening. Leslie has been in today and had a cooked dinner and tonight he'll have a snack. They used to have all their breakfast cereals in the house but Leslie especially doesn't know when to stop – so they haven't even got a toaster because if they had Leslie would eat the whole lot himself. He can eat a whole loaf of bread and he eats things out of my freezer. So I just take away the opportunity so we don't have the problem. Breakfast they collect as well.

He didn't do that at Wentwood but I suppose someone was on duty all the time. On Sunday do you have a cooked lunch?

Yes, they prefer to eat theirs in their house and sometimes I cook in there and we eat in there with them.

What time do they get up on Sunday? Any time they like – sometimes 12 o'clock. *What happens if they want to stay in bed all day?*

I don't agree with that – I'd never let them stay in bed all day. I think it's terrible – a waste of your life.

Do you keep any food in their house? No not even biscuits, they come in to me for biscuits.

Do they do any house work?

No. The cleaning things were in here but the cleaner's taken them home with her because they were getting lost. They don't do any gardening either – their concentration isn't good enough.

Who decides when they get up?

They're very good – if they've not come over for their breakfast I come and call them. They've got to come and get it.

Who buys his clothes? I do *Does he choose any himself?*

Sometimes but he doesn't like shopping. I normally go, like I've just bought him a jacket. I know what he likes.

Have you ever tried taking him with you? Yes – we don't get anywhere. *What about shopping, do you buy the food?* Yes. *Do they ever help?* Not usually, I do it all. *Who chose the furniture?*

I did. They've got a phone in here but I don't encourage them to use it. They go out to use the phone up the road but Leslie can't dial the number so I do it for him.

Has he got a key? No. *He's got a key to his mum's house – will he ever get locked out?* No, there's always somebody in here. *Has he got a key to his bedroom?* No.

They're out two nights at clubs and on a Friday night my girls go roller skating. We used to take Leslie and the others to the pub part of the rink as they didn't want to roller skate. They'd sit and watch but now they are going to go to Gateway. I've got reservations about the club so I've got to go and see what its like now.

I do all the banking for them all. I get it out of the Post Office and give him what he needs each day. They've all got bank accounts. Leslie has got a habit of spending his bus fare and he has to walk home and it's a long way to walk from town to here. I've done quite a bit of work with him over the year. I just sit him down with my kids and we learn money together but his concentration is very bad.

I think it's terrible money for care in the community when you think that you get less per hour than a child minder does and yet the responsibility is so much greater. I don't do it for the money. The thing was I had no social life. I was working in a mental hospital which was quite depressing so I used to bring them all home for the weekend when I worked in the mental hospital. My husband said you can't do that you've got to have a separate life – which I've got now – I've got the children.

The parents

I'd had his name down with MENCAP for years and he left Wentwood and the obvious thing would have been for him to have left Wentwood and gone into somewhere like that, but it didn't work out like that. He was home for a year and nothing happened so I decided to chase everybody up. So we said what else is there? So they started to search round and they came up with that. An opportunity came up at MEN-CAP when they they were converting a house for three or four bedsits but it wouldn't have been run by a family it would have been run by staff.

These social workers don't always tell you the whole truth; they seem to hold things back – if you want to find out anything you find out things from parents not social workers. We didn't want his sister to feel she was responsible for him – we had a word with her and told her. Somebody said to me years ago – don't you ever worry about Leslie there'll always be somebody to look after him. I was told that at school and I've carried that with me all the time.

The house is far more active there, far more taking place over there than here. There's only me and mother here. He missed the company. He has our company but its not the same, is it. When Leslie went over there first we said that's going to be his new home provided it worked out all right. The welfare worker found it for him. Going to Wentwood got him to meet other people. He used to get out and about everywhere and he had a very active social life there which when he came home it just ended – because we haven't got a social life. He kept wanting to phone them up when he first came home – it was murder. He used to say 'Mum I'm missing my friends' and I'd ring them up, but we used to have to judge it when they were there.

Are you happy with the home? Well it wouldn't be my scene but he's quite happy there.

She says he eats the food if it's left out, has he always done that? Oh yes. *He didn't do it at Wentwood.*

He was under far greater supervision there, much closer supervision. Now the aim is for independence although Leslie has never really achieved that.

What do you do with him here over the weekend about food? Keep an eye on him. *Is it a battle all the time?*

Not really. If there's a big packet of crisps in the drawer he'll go backwards and forwards eating them all, but when we say that's enough Leslie, he stops. But if she left it in the house where Leslie and the others are she wouldn't be there to say no and when the food is gone it's too late to say no. It's crisps or sausage rolls or pork pies, mainly savoury things that he can eat.

Who buys Leslie clothes? Leslie. *She said she did.*

Well Leslie supplies the money and they go together because when he lived at home he always went in with us to choose them.

What did you hope Wentwood would do for him?

Gain more independence. What we really wanted was not total independence but to be able to run his life as best as possible when we've gone.

Another similar placement visited, where two residents were living in one large house with a caring and efficient young lady of much the same age as themselves, was most successful. Social Services were regular and supportive visitors and it appeared to be a sympathetic placement for a somewhat hyperactive ex-student who was happy and well settled there.

Angela
Possibly the most disturbing interview of the research was with Angela, aged 26, a very able lady with Down's syndrome who left Wentwood with the highest final assessment score of all the ex-students. Although she had only increased by three skills over the years there was little advance she could have made on her Wentwood leaving score and unusually she had retained all her skills. Angela had lived totally independently for six years in a supported housing scheme run by a voluntary organisation. The house was shared by two able residents who worked in the locality and three developmentally disabled ladies. Having achieved the 'blueprint' of care in the community and the so called 'ordinary life', she was far from happy. She also appeared to be affected by the *laissez faire* that was prevalent in ladies with Down's syndrome in the sample.

After leaving Wentwood Angela completed a work experience placement in a catering establishment for people with learning disabilities, which gave her an excellent training in catering and she thoroughly enjoyed her work in the attached cafe. She learnt quickly, was well thought of and her progress reports contained words like *exemplary* and *excellent* in every area. Her training was still in evidence some years later where, in her own fridge, she had a range of homemade foods which looked most appetizing.

After work experience Angela completed a two year special needs course in a local college of education where she had just embarked on a third year. Angela arrived back from college just in time for the interview and on her way up to her room had answered the phone twice, writing down messages for other people and collecting a written one already left for her. She had a private phone and phone number in her room. She could read and write fairly well, belonged to the local library and was completely self-sufficient when shopping for her needs.

The house was in a poor decorative state and there were many items broken. During the visit it was noted that amongst other things the toilet seat was off, curtains in Angela room were falling down and her chest of drawers was broken. She said they had been like that for years! There was a house meeting one night a week where the key worker involved with the project dealt with housekeeping money, household rotas and other problems such as vetinary treatment for the cat.

When the interviewer approached the key-worker by phone she was told that the residents were independent and although occasional voluntary workers maintained some contact there was no further professional support. The key worker also pointed out that that any arrangements must be made with Angela herself, who lived a totally independent life. Almost certainly, if the residents had thought to mention the dilapidated state of the building at the weekly meeting repairs would have been carried out by the management.

Initially, after leaving Wentwood, Angela had good support from key workers to help her settle in and records exist from this time. Social skills were well documented, as was her progress at work. Uniquely, to this study, assessment and documentation were excellent and much thought had obviously been given to introducing her to various local community provisions and women's groups. Records indicate that Angela was so busy with work and leisure activities that she had little time to see her key worker. A plea was made in the records for Angela to stay in at least every other Saturday so the key worker could take her to practise shopping for clothes.

Initially, Angela made regular weekend visits to her parents, who were separated, but as shown in the interview below she no longer wished to maintain this contact

At Wentwood you did work experience, what did you do when you left Wentwood? Catering. *What did you make?* Everything, all the salad, pea soup, coleslaw. *Did you work in the cafe?* Yes – *did you like it?* Yes I liked it there but I did two years then I finished.

Do you ever go out for a meal now? Oh no, it's too expensive. *Don't you go with your mum or dad* – I live here now, I go shopping with myself. *Do you ever go for a meal to McDonalds or anywhere?*

No, – it's a bit podgy – too much chips. I do like them hamburgers but when I was ill I called at McDonalds.

You've had glandular fever haven't you? I did yes. *Are you feeling better now?*

Joy said said I should eat at McDonalds. It's not up to Joy (Dad's friend). Some people who have been here a long time they're starting to move out. I've been here six years.

Do you want to move out? I do yes. *Where do you want go?*

I don't know, where I can be happy. I went to Home Farm Trust. I went there but I was half asleep. On my first day they said do you want to go to the Home Farm Trust and I said, I do yes – and we were arguing about it with dad.

Did you win? They said it was too big for me. *Do you think it's too big?* I dunno – well yes it is.

Would you like to go there?

> I would yes because there's more to do – it's out of London it's in the South.

And where would you want to live if you move out of here? You don't have to move – but what sort of place would you like? Somewhere there are more people so they can't have a go at you. *Why can't they have a go at you?* Because they've got staff there.

I see, you mean that if there's somewhere where there's staff that's better, so they can't have a go at you. Would you rather be somewhere with staff? I don't know if I will be happy there. It's difficult isn't it to know what to do?

Would you like to be somewhere where there are staff there all the time. I don't know, staff can shout at people. *Staff can shout at people?* Oh yes, if you do something wrong staff shout at you. *Where have been where staff shouted at you?*

> At B... if you do things properly they won't shout. It's big. I might be happy there and have my money myself. I think it's all wrong to stop my book like that.

Did you tell them? um – um – *who stopped it.* Eric took it a long time ago, it's in the office and I still haven't got it. If I want any money I ask. I've got money – I've got £20. *Where did that come from?* Tuesday money – *is that when you have your house meeting on Tuesday?* Yes. *What do you do? Who cleans the house* – we do it all. *Is there a list* – yes up here.

I want my money book. *If you went to B... would they give you your book?* No. *Did you ask them when you went there for the day?* Yes – they'll give you your own wages on Friday. *How much would the wages be – did you ask?* I didn't. *Do your mum and dad give you money?* No – never – No.

How do you manage with change when you give money – do you find it difficult? I do yes – *very difficult?* I do yes *have you got a bus pass* yes *when you shop at Sainsbury's and it comes to paying for it do you know how much change you should get or not?* No, I dunno. I'm getting better actually with the money – *are you?* I am.

Were you having difficulty with the money?

> I did before yes – I'm hopeless. They took my book away and they said stop screaming – when you can stop screaming you can have your book back.

When did you scream?

> When they gave me my book to do. Why are you screaming for they said. I said, I dunno – for attention.

And were you? Yes.

Did you like Wentwood? Yes I did. *Where would you be happier living?*

Good question – how long for? I've been here far too long – I likes Wentwood better.

Better than here? I did yes. *Is that because there were staff?* Yes. *You like having staff?* I do yes. *Why?*

To work with you. The last year at Wentwood I was working with Ann and I was working with myself.

You enjoyed working with the staff? I did yes. *Did you like the cafe with the staff after you left Wentwood?* I did yes

So you'd really like to go somewhere where they have staff like at Wentwood? Yes.

Most people would think it was very good to be here looking after yourself.

I know. It's hard work you know. Like if you're sick or something – what would you do? Stay in bed?

I think so, what would you do?

Stay in bed and sleep – how can I come downstairs and cook for myself if I'm sick?

You can't. No I can't. *And you think that's what's wrong with this place?* Yes it is. *You were ill a long time with glandular fever weren't you?* Yes I was.

I think that's the phone ringing.

I know. I live here, and that phone keeps ringing, and it was me answered last time – and every time.

Let somebody else take it, everybody else is in! OK. *Do you want to answer it?* No I don't. *If you wait long enough, it's only a question of waiting and somebody else will answer it.* OK.

I'm very interested, perhaps you can tell me – there's something I've wondered about a lot and I don't know the answer – this business of staff – do you think staff are a good thing? Is it nice to have them around if you're ill –

If you're very ill you tell the whole truth without playing up. Sometimes I do play up and start to be silly.

I think you're very sensible

When I had that diarrhoea they said don't be so silly – but you can't help diarrhoea.

No you can't. Did you have tummy ache? Yes. *Did you eat something that upset you?* Off milk. *Is that why you were looking at the top of the milk for the date*

when you made your tea? Yes I did. When I cook for myself I give myself too much food. *Do you feel ill after that?* I do yes

Do you not know that you've got too much food until you've finished eating it?

Yes I do. Like today I had rice crispies, macaroni cheese and chips for lunch at college. I shouldn't have chips actually and macaroni cheese and baked beans and salad.

You can have them but it's rather a lot and with salad! Perhaps you could have had the macaroni cheese and salad and beans and not the chips, or just the chips. Would you like to be able to ask somebody sometimes questions like that?

Does chips go with macaroni cheese – I don't think it does actually!

Is there any thing else that worries you? College. *Do you go every day –*

I find it too much. I find it too much to go every day and I don't have half term at college. Last year I done two years at college –

Is it a class for people who have special needs and need to learn special things? That's right, yes. *Do you like it?*

Yes but it's too much going every day when I've done two years. I've been doing too much – I did it. They gave me a time to go at 11 o'clock this year – it's not really up to them to say that, it's up to me. I get very tired. I don't like rushing.

Hang on a minute – do you think there are too many people telling you what to do? Yes there are. Yes.

That's what it sounds like. I know.

Wherever you go is somebody telling you what to do? Yes they are – *and what would you like to do about that?*

I've done my two years there and now they're nagging me at 11 o'clock –

Would you like to stop going – yes I would. *You don't want to go any more?*

No, I've done two years there and we used to finish at quarter to three and now we don't finish until half past.

And how long does it take you to get home – not long at all We do cooking and I like that. We used to start at 10 o'clock and we worked on our own and we had lunch at 12.15. We had to wash up at half past twelve and could leave at twenty to one. Guess what time we got home –

I don't know, what time? One o'clock. *You don't like college –* some of it no – *are you sick of going – has it been too long?* Yes.

What would you like to do?

> When Edith said you're going to a last year at college I should have said no in the first place.

Did you say yes to begin with? I didn't at first no – *but she persuaded you?* Yes she did. *Who was Edith?* She was my key worker – and now I've got another one.

Would you like to be somewhere where you didn't have to go out to college and there was a lot going on – like Wentwood – did you like that sort of life?

> I did yes – Edith persuaded me to go to college and I said no. I didn't want to go. She persuaded me.

Does everyone go out all day here? No – *if you hadn't gone to college what would you have done?*

> Well it's up to me. Write letters to people – what's wrong with that?

Nothing – I'll give you my address and you can write to me if you'd like to – I will yes.

If you're unhappy and things go wrong who do you tell? My key worker Joan. *How often does she come here –* on Thursdays and Tuesdays.

I spoke to Joan on the phone and she said you were very independent and she did very little for you. She said you did everything by yourself.

What are you doing at Christmas? I dunno. *Are you staying here?* I can't. *Why?* There's nobody here – *but you live here.* I can't if the others go home and they're going home.

Do you want to go and see your Mum and Dad at Christmas – not really, no. *Have you ever stayed here on your own in the house?*

> I get lonely in the house – no-one to talk to. I don't know what I'll do at Christmas.

The input by all the relevant agencies into Angela's life has been impeccable. She benefited from her training at Wentwood where from a low score on entry, her final score indicated that she had very few skills left to gain. Whilst there she also did a long work experience placement for 52 weeks at a public house and restaurant and another one for a shorter time at a private nursing home. Both employers were delighted with her and wrote glowing reports.

After leaving Wentwood, Angela was fortunate to attend a full catering course and a then two year further education course with the option of a third year. Both were specially designed for people with learning disabilities. She was the recipient of unusually thorough training when she moved into her independent living provision in a pleasant residential area ideally sited in close proximity to shops and public transport. She attended several clubs and women's groups and was taken by taxi each week to a well known drama course with opportunities for people with learning difficulties to integrate with their more able peers. Everybody from every agency appeared to be delighted with her progress.

However, the third year at college doing cookery, about which she was complaining, appeared to be at a lower level than the catering course she had completed some three years before. It would appear that her complaints were valid and that she had been persuaded to undertake the third year more for administrative convenience than for her own benefit.

It would be difficult to improve on the caring back-up Angela had received over the years from the people involved with her progress. Both her parents had maintained contact and took her on holidays – although her description of her relationship with her family contained (from her point of view) several recent stressful episodes. She had the insight to realise that these were in some measure due to her own inadequacies and her inability to complain when they hurt her feelings.

Life over the past six years, while outwardly successful, had become increasingly barren and lonely. The residents of the house were unable to sustain any social life and much of her time was spent in her room eating her solitary meals that she had so carefully cooked. It appeared that nobody ate in the large bleak kitchen but either retired to their rooms with a tray or ate with the tray on their knee while watching television in the lounge.

She was attending a course that she found too tiring and slightly unnecessary and was about to go on an expensive holiday with a religious organisation she disliked and considered a waste of her own money. Yet again she had been persuaded that she would enjoy it and for want of any better option had been unable to say no. On top of all this she didn't know what to do for Christmas. For the interviewer, the contrast between Angela's plight and the excitement of the rest of the ex-students, as they prepared for Christmas in their family or group homes, was very sad.

Unlike some of the other ex-students in the sample Angela did not shun the company of her disabled peers but actively enjoyed such contacts. She also valued the authority of 'staff' who in her experience had many useful functions. Possibly, unrealised by her, their most important function was to help her find the sort of communal pleasures that her more fortunate peers, including her own brothers, enjoyed as part of their affinity with the outside world.

Angela also demonstrated a surprising amount of common sense. The author inadvertently left a watch on Angela's bed and when sending the statutory 'thank you' card also asked if she had found it – suggesting that if found, she would ring her next time she was in the area and collect it. Angela had asked for an address to write a letter to the author and had been given a card. Before any further phone calls could be made the watch arrived through the post – in a very thin envelope – somewhat problematically addressed, but with the post code clearly written.

(Shortly after the interview Angela chose to relinquish her hard earned independence and live in a fully staffed community for people with developmental disabilities. Here, as she had already ascertained, she is assured of waged work, a social life in the company of both staff and peers, and a home for the rest of her life if she so chooses.)

Brian

Brian, aged 28, was the only student living independently in a council flat on his own. He was not over bright but after a low final assessment at Wentwood he had increased his score by 14 life skills over the years. His life is dealt with more fully in Chapter 5 but these aspects of his daily life illustrate how tenuous such independence is. Brian's key worker lived nearby and used to be a home help. She had complete control of his life and he was totally dependent on her and her husband. They have accepted him into their life at what must be some cost to their own privacy.

Brian has had a somewhat chequered career and his current life style sounds a vast improvement to his earlier years. His parents were doubtful if he would be prepared to be interviewed and doubted that he would be able to give much information. As shown in Chapter 5, social workers held a somewhat jaundiced view of him. Wentwood records also indicated disruptive and difficult behaviour. Brian lived alone and had no friends or visitors other than his key worker. Helped by a trip to the pub, the conversation went on, at Brian's request, for a couple hours. Several topics met the response 'we don't talk about that'. Mabel confirmed the accuracy of what was said about his current life.

> I've got a neighbour called Mabel, she's helped me since I come here, she's helped me a lot. You see I had trouble back here a long time ago. This girl, she wasted all my life and I used to know this man called Keith. I did his housework a long time ago. He was horrid man he did my life in. Mabel's helped me a lot. I had some problems two years ago with this girl.

What happened with the girl?

> She led me into serious trouble. We came into here and we went in a car and the police caught me and I got into serious trouble. She said to me, let's do it. We went to H— and the police took me to home to my Mum's place.

And what did she say? What are you doing here? Was the girl with you?

> No they took her back to her place and my mum took me back she did and we don't talk about it.

Can you read? A bit, not much. *You don't ever have any money at all?* Mabel keeps it for me – *but when she's away like now how do you get some money?* My pocket money. *Where's your pocket money?* I get it tomorrow, out of that money. *Do you go to the post office and get your allowance?* No I don't. *Who gets it for you?* Mabel does.

Do you find money difficult? Yes. *Have you got a bus pass?* No. *How do you pay?* I ask how much is and they tell me. *How much is it?* er... *How do you pay?* I give them £2. *Do you know what sort of change you get?* No. *Can't you work it out?* To go back to my sports, I love watching boxing. I saw it on Sky 2 o'clock in the morning last weekend. I slept at Mabel's house. *Do you sleep there at weekends?* Just sometimes.

I go to college. *Where?* To see my teacher. Home lessons at Mabel's. *Oh! You go Mabel's house like college – she's your teacher?* Yes. *When?* Any time I want to. *What do you learn?* Reading and spelling. *What about money and number?* –

Who buys your clothes? Mabel does. *Do buy any yourself?* My Mother buys them sometimes. *Do you ever go and buy any yourself?* No. I'm not allowed to have the money. *Why – you might spend it on something else?* Yes. *Who buys your food?* Mabel does. *You don't have any money for food?* No. *Do you go together?* Yes. *You don't have any money?* No. *What happens if you want to have a drink, haven't you any money for that?* No she handles it. *I've got money today so it's OK. What happens if you want to buy a bar of chocolate, does Mabel give you the money every day?* We collect my money at a place every Thursday.

When you're unhappy and you had these tempers (that we're not talking about) who do you tell? Mabel – if I've got problems I don't tell my Mum. *How long has Mabel been with you?* Three years. *That's a long time.*

Is there anything you want to do that you can't? I want to go on a big holiday by myself – *by your self not with Mabel?* With my Dad – my real Dad in the States. *Oh your Dad is in the States is he?* We don't talk about that. I went on holiday with Mabel and her husband. She's got two puppies– *you didn't take them did you?* Yes she's got a caravan. *Did you like it?* Yes. *What did you do?* Lots. *What did you like doing best?* Walking – just walking.

What do you do when Mabel's on holiday? Somebody comes called Ann. *Is she nice?* Yes – *and they come every day?* Yes. *What would you do if they didn't come?* Starve! Starve to death. *I don't believe that for one minute, how far away does she live?* Not far.

[On the way to the pub Brian pins a note to an outside locker]

What's that for? I get my lunch Tuesday and Thursday. *What time do they come?* 12 o'clock. *Isn't it going to get cold?* No I heat it up.

[We meet the lady delivering dinner on the way out and she puts it in the locker.]

Being independent is quite difficult, isn't it. If you hadn't put that notice up what would have happened? I wouldn't have got my lunch bringed.

Don't you buy any of your clothes? No, Mabel does, I'm not interested. *What happens if your shoes need repairing?* Get some new shoes. *You don't get them mended?* No. Mum sends money for hair cuts. *What would you do about haircuts if mum didn't send you money?* Look scruffy, Mabel says I look scruffy. *You've got a beautiful bubble cut who did that for you?* A lady just down the road. It costs £4.

Mabel helped me a lot. *Did she?* Yes she's changed my life. *What's she done that's made it change?* She get me in the church football team. *What else has Mabel done that changed your life?* Running, she got me into the running club. *She's very nice to you isn't she?* And Jim. *Do you ever help him?* Wash his car for him.

Are you going to see my Mum? *Yes but she's away.* Next time you see her will you tell her she's done well with me? *Your Mum or Mabel.* Both.

Mary

Mary, aged 24, was a small lady with Down's syndrome and a congenital dislocation of the hip. A little overweight, she dressed in an all enveloping track suit. Although not one of the highest scoring ex-students on her final assessment she had gained five further living skills. Mary had such incredible verbal ability and confidence that her story was treated with some suspicion, appearing to be more phantasy than reality. Luckily, the interviewer went along with her life story – with some amusement – only to find that on talking to her mother Mary had painted a true and accurate picture of her life. She lived on a newly built housing estate with Jean, a lady of similar ability, in a MENCAP Supported Living project. The new semi-detached house was attached to an identical one which housed three men in similar living conditions. Support staff came in nightly for a couple of hours to help with the evening meal. The house was beautifully kept by the two ladies, who were very proud of it and this particular supported living project worked particularly well, managing to counter the loneliness found in other similar projects. However, it proved impossible to contact any of the support staff, even after several attempts, which was a common feature of such houses. Mary had managed all the arrangements and correspondence regarding the interview herself and, as people came and went freely in both houses, had possibly not informed anybody of the visit. Mary visits her family every other weekend and sleeps at home. An independent traveller, she is able to move freely about a rather isolated area and takes buses both to her home and to the nearest town.

Did you want to come here? Yes I did – *Did your mum want you to?* I don't know. *Do your family come and see you here?*

> Yes they do. I've got two sisters and three brothers [rattles off names] and I've got mum and dad – my dad is lovely he's tall, he's handsome, he's good looking – they're both divorced. I haven't seem him for ages. I'm the youngest of my family.

What do you like about living here because you're very independent, I haven't met many people from Wentwood who are living like this. I just like it, it's fine. *You don't get lonely?* No I never get lonely and I've split up with my boyfriend. I've got my friends.

You not lived here long have you because when I wrote to you, you were living with your mum? Yes I was – *and you're living all by yourself –* yes I'm independent. *Your mum must be very proud of you* – I think she is. I'm 24 now.

Were you and Jean friends before? Yes. *Did you used to go to the centre together?* Yes but I don't go now. *What do you do?* I go to the leisure centre – *what do you do there?* Exercise, swimming, keep fit, sometimes cricket. *Do you just go by yourself?*

> No some from next door goes, three boys live there and us two here, we live here and the staff come in during the day. No staff sleep here.

Do you go to Gateway?

> No I don't never go to Gateway. There's a club at the leisure centre where they do table tennis, bowls, darts.

Do you ever go to the pub?

> Yes I do sometimes with my family, sometimes the staff go with us. Sometimes we go and have a drink don't we Jean? Sometimes we go by staff car, sometimes by taxi – the staff order it.

Who does the cooking? We take it in turns and the shopping. *Do you do it all yourself?* Sometimes the staff helps you – sometimes we forget to do the shopping sometimes.

So what happens, do you have house meetings with staff?

> No we don't, the boys next door do. I like sewing – like if I rip my clothes I sew them. Sometimes I can't do it very well. Sometimes if it's a pigsty this house I clean it. Sometimes I have a lie in bed if I feel tired.

Can you tell the time? Only a little bit, not a lot. *You haven't even got a clock here have you. How do you know when it's time for tea?* It depends how you feel isn't it? *You don't have it at any particular time?* Sometimes we have it at six o'clock. *Is that when the staff come in to help?* Yes – we take it in turns to help.

What time do you go to bed? Whenever I want. *Do the staff come and see if you're in bed?* No. *Do they make sure you get up?* No. *If you're unhappy or something goes wrong here who do you tell?* The staff.

Who is going to do this big garden? We do not know. *You're not going to?* No, I'm not going to, men do that bit, it's not women's job – we're not as strong as them. I do my own washing and my own ironing.

You don't go to the centre any more, when did you stop going?

I only stopped it because it's too much for me – too busy. *Is it too noisy?* No it's not noisy but it's just too much and it's too isolated and it's a long way from here.

Where is it? P— I've just come from there it's in the middle of nowhere, I got lost there. *Do you like not going to the centre?* Yes I like it, I like it here.

Did you like Wentwood? I do. *What did you like about it?* I used to write letters to my mum. We did very hard work there with my files. *Did you like that?* I did yes – *but you don't like going to the centre do you?* No – *but you did like the hard work at Wentwood?* Yes I did. *What was different?* It's just different that's all. *Would you like to be doing things now like at Wentwood because you liked the hard work?* It's very hard to describe isn't it – very hard. *Is life better here than it was at Wentwood?* I'm quite happy here, I wouldn't go back there.

Have you got a boyfriend?

I used to he was John Black. I was engaged but we split up. We had a lot of rows and arguments and it didn't work out it didn't work out properly. I split up with my boyfriend in February. I used to live with him in Cross Street. The trouble is with men they can be a pain in the arse.

So who else lived in the house? That's it. *Just the two of you?* Yes. *How long did you live with him for?* A fairly long time.

Where did you meet him? He met me down in the centre. Before summer we first met. *Did your mum say you could live with him?* No, we both did.

Was your mother quite happy about you living with him?

Very hard to describe. She did want it – well how can I put it. She did, but she wasn't very happy. My family didn't like him because he's thick in the head. He said lots of things – be horrible to me. I was horrible to him myself.

How old was he, your age?

No he was a granddad. You see he had grey hair, I don't know how old he is – I don't know.

Would you like another boyfriend? Not just yet I don't feel like rushing yet. *If you had another boyfriend would you like to live in the same house as him?* NO WAY.

Did you have any staff sort of looking after you? We had a social worker. *What did she do – did they just come in at night for an hour like here?* Yes they did.

How you do work the money out here – where do you get it from? We have to go to the Post Office. We have a pension book and we have to sign it. *Do you go on your own?* Sometimes the staff comes with us. *Do you pay rent here?* Yes we have to work it all out. The staff help. *How much pocket money do you get?* We get one bit of money to last all week unless we're doing Christmas shopping. *Who goes with you?* My keyworker.

Is there anything here you would like to do living here, or can't do here? It's very hard to decide isn't it? *Is there anything you would like to do but you haven't the money or you can't do it?* I don't get problems like that – *aren't you lucky!*

Mother

What did Wentwood do for her?

She got the confidence at Wentwood. There was not a lot to offer where she was. There was nothing to offer except the centre and that wasn't that good at that particular time. She went to the special school from three years old and left it at seventeen. They gave her her hygiene. I thought her hygiene was good before she went but it wasn't. They also taught her independence, like using the buses and transport which we hadn't done. She went to Bath on her own. There would be somebody to meet her there. When we would go down she would take us out on the bus to a pub in the country and know exactly where to get off. They were fantastic. When she got back home she would go off down town on her own. Of course I'd never let her I'd be so scared that she would get on the wrong bus but she can go in and out on her own now. They gave her her independence.

Why she stopped going to the centre was that when she met up with this boyfriend, he hated it, because he had been there since he was a child going back into the forties I think. He put it into her head how wicked it was over there. Of course when he was young they didn't have the skills and he was 45. He hated it there and he turned her against it. I didn't want her to leave there because they had so much to offer. She loved the staff but she just stopped and that's it and she's never gone back. I got one of the staff to come over and have a chat with her and she still didn't want to but she's very happy. She loves the horse riding and all the other things she does. She works at the

Co-op one day on a YTS scheme, goes to the leisure centre two days, goes riding one day and does pottery at college one day.

Did she get married? No thank God. *She said she went over your head and 'the both of us decided'.* Yes that's quite right. *Did she actually go over your head?* Yes she did, that's true, I knocked it, I didn't think they were – it shouldn't be allowed that is how I feel.

Why shouldn't they be allowed?

Well I thought they weren't capable of love. They didn't know the value of money. OK, she knew how to cook but she came from a big family and of course we cook for six people and of course she never saw me cook a little bit for one or two. However, so she did go over my head to social services and they told me off. They said why should she not live on her own – I'd made mistakes, they said she would make mistakes and learn from them, I thought, well that is true, we all make our mistakes and she was 21.

Did you have the power ultimately to stop it? No because she was over age. *It's quite a frightening thought really isn't it?*

It's very frightening. We had to pick the pieces up. They moved into this very big flat up three flights of stairs. They set up home and we all helped – she had a dislocated hip and she had all those stairs up to the flat. Anyway they set up home and I had a very great liaison with the social worker – and we arranged she would go one day and I would go another.

You went every other day?

I really was a nervous wreck. The flat was lovely and they had it lovely. He would do the washing once a week – no tumbler drier – nowhere to dry in the winter. They couldn't put it out anywhere so they had a horse to put it out on and a pulley line in the bathroom. Then when it was damp they would put it away in the drawer damp!

Then they would shop – and they would shop and it would be about £45. They had a massive freezer which was choc-a-block. They would have a massive breakfast in the morning, lunch at 12 o'clock and sometimes they would have afternoon tea. A cooked supper and in between sometimes they would go out for a meal. Mary was 15 stone in the end and she was only 8 stone when she first went in. She's 10 stone now and it's gradually going off.

How long did all this go on for?

They moved in a week before the Easter '91 and it lasted until February '92. In between that they had terrible rows – awful rows. I think they used to run out of money when they'd go shopping and of course she used to make an awful shout and fuss, and of course she would walk out of the shop, so she said, and he had to put some of the stuff back.

Did he have any sense of money? I honestly don't know. *Did you like him?*

He was a very gentle man but she was the one with the temper. He would shout and create like that verbally but she would hit him. Once he was decorating. So I thought, 'Oh God, I'll help' and I said to him OK 'I'll come down this Tuesday'. They had the living room down because they were going to do the bedroom. I said, 'I'll take the paint and the brushes and what have you down,' and the three of us would get cracking and we'd have it done in one day. I went down this day and John said 'I can't help you I've got a bad back'. He looked as if he was in agony so I put a cushion on the bed which was in the sitting room then, and propped him up and put him on the bed and got him some pain killers. In the meantime Ann the social worker came in and I said 'hey – you know you mustn't do this' but she'd had a phone call from one of their neighbours saying there was an almighty row coming from their flat and would somebody investigate. Mary was still out at the shops and John was in bed and he'd never said anything to me except he had a bad back. So Ann said 'what's the matter John?' and he said **'I want to go in a safe place'.**

Apparently Mary took him a cup of tea in bed and he didn't respond so she threw him out of bed and as he fell out he banged some part of his body. He banged his back on the side of the bed as he went down and some other part of his anatomy on whatever piece of furniture was beside the bed. Then when he tried to stand up, she kicked him. Of course by this time she was 15 stone – yes she packed quite a punch and John was scared to death and just wanted to go to safe place.

Did she have a temper at home?

Oh yes she had the outbursts but she wouldn't punch or anything. But I think the whole thing – the sexual intimacy, the shopping – everything – but most of all was the intimacy, was too much. I can't get her to talk about it

Ann said she would have to take John to hospital because he was hurt and Mary said 'I would like to go as well' and Ann said 'no' and Mary tried to push Ann away to get to John but he said 'No I need a break from you Mary.' He was a gentle man, he never did anything but she used to thump hell out of him. I couldn't believe it. Both Ann and I, we met afterwards and we just couldn't believe it. She never wanted to leave him, he wanted to leave her to go in a safe place. Anyway they moved him away. He was a gentle man but of course he was much too old for Mary.

What would you have done if she had children?

God only knows. She was very good with taking the pill.

She said her brothers didn't like him. They were very protective towards her, we all are. Maybe this was why they just didn't like to see her be hurt.

How did they get to go the social workers themselves to overrule you? She just went down there to Social Services. *How did she know where to go?* That I don't know. I honestly don't know. I wouldn't have had a clue.

I think too in the flat where they were, she didn't go out anywhere. At the beginning she used to go two days a week to the centre and then because he didn't like it she stopped. He didn't go anywhere, he didn't have any kind of work or anywhere to go so they were there all day and all night. I don't think that helped either, they had no outlets.

She came home in the February and she was very quiet, very withdrawn for a while. We took her here, there and everywhere – bought her a new wardrobe and new clothes. My son took her for a weekend. Little things like that. I think social services are very good and there are a lot of little group homes in the area but I'm glad we were here for her.

Where she is now, have you got what you want for her? Not really. *What do you want?*

Ideally I think she needs support. She does need that and also she does need her independence. Ideally it would be in a family environment, more than she is now with just the two of them. Jean has done her own thing, she's got a boyfriend and Mary comes home every other weekend. I don't know if I would want her to live with a family because I have seen a lot of that and that doesn't work. I think they are downtrodden because a lot of people don't understand them. They've just opened a group home where they've got flats for couples who can't function on their own. They have a full staff there and it is beautifully run. There is a lovely atmosphere there.

I worry about when I'm not here. I really do. I worry about then.

DISCUSSION
The Home Group
The majority of people in the family home were not as happy or outgoing as the people in the other two groups. They had few, if any, friends of their own age and their social life tended to be limited to older relatives and friends of the family. Parents usually said during the interview how much their off-

spring enjoyed contact with these relatives but careful questioning of family members revealed that often their son or daughter would retreat to a different part of the house during such visits.

With one or two exceptions there was very little opportunity for people living at home to practise or develop self-help skills. In most families it appeared to be the norm for mother to do the bulk of the washing, cleaning and cooking and father to do the gardening and do-it-yourself jobs. When there were other siblings still living at home they too did very little in the house, so in this way the developmentally disabled peer could not be said to be discriminated against. However, their plight became more apparent when the other siblings had left the family home.

Most homes had a tried and tested routine that allowed such things to be done with the minimum of fuss, especially where family members worked and time was at a premium. One father, who had two other teenage siblings living at home, echoed the feelings of many other parents after years of trying to get his ex-Wentwood son to do something other than stay in bed all day

> I'm sure he could get up to get out in the afternoon but in reality it's a working household with other people to consider and we've got to the state now that if there's no hassle – it's worth a lot.

The conversations above illustrate problems found in all the families where ex-students still lived at home. Their place within the home appeared to have remained like that of a dependent child and quite dissimilar to that of their adult siblings. Those people who had been able to capitalise on the travel skills they had been taught were able to enjoy an independent working life, however restricted their home life appeared to be.

Although people living in group homes were being introduced to the concepts of self advocacy and empowerment – even if such concepts were imperfectly understood – there seemed to be no such mechanism in place for people living at home. The minority of parents had some, rather minimal, contact with a key-worker but it appeared that key-workers were hesitant to become involved in family life. Parents were often unsure of either the name or the role of the key-worker. Many of the interviews reflected this uncertainty and it became apparent that key-workers tended to limit contact with the client living in the family home to either visits to a centre during the day, or meeting away from the family home for some sort of outing. Very rarely did a key-worker have regular contact with the home. This did not happen when clients were living independently or in a group home. Here the role of the key-worker was well understood and very much appreciated by the client when questioned. In many cases the key-worker was the only 'significant other' clients could relate to and, as such, was the key figure in their lives.

There was evidence of a level of control within the family that may well have been unacceptable if applied by staff in group homes. Due to parental intervention several of the women had their menstruation stopped by various means. In every case there was clear evidence in the Wentwood records that they had been taught how to cope with their periods or, if they had arrived at Wentwood without such expertise, they had left coping well. A number of women had also undergone hysterectomies and were not clear about the need for, or implications of, this operation. Women in group homes who had undergone various similar procedures had usually done so before leaving the parental home. Two women in group homes had medical symptoms that necessitated such invasive techniques.

On the death of their parents, people living at home will almost certainly have to move to some type of community provision, where yet again they they will retrain in all the skills they mastered at Wentwood. Henrietta Reynolds, their principal at Wentwood, made strong recommendations that the majority of students should not return to the family home after leaving Wentwood but should move directly into whatever type of suitable semi-independent living provision their local authority could provide. Those students who went to a group home immediately on leaving Wentwood and those who subsequently requested that they should be allowed to live semi-independent lives away from their families, do not seem to have suffered any ill effects from the consequences of their decisions. Some people living a more independent life away from home were often unhappy, but even they had no wish to return to live with their families and appeared to favour a move to a more enclosed community which offered them a pleasant social life and the company of a similar peer group.

SALIENT ISSUES
Professionals
Key workers are needed by the clients living at home to ensure that they have an opportunity to discuss problems arising from their home life. A proportion of the work should be carried out within the family home so that the key-worker keeps in contact with the family and is able to estimate the validity of problems. It would be helpful if key workers wrote to families giving their name, a contact number, and explaining their role, because it was clear in this research most families had no idea of the role of the key worker.

Throughout the interviews the ex-students gave clear and accurate information about their lives at Wentwood, verified by checking the records or asking Wentwood staff. As seen from the transcripts, most people were well able to talk about their lives and what made them happy or unhappy. Tara's key-worker was unusual in that sensing problems in Tara's home life, rather than antagonise the father she used her time to take them both in her car to do the weekly shopping at what was probably a difficult and unsocial hour. Even then, the father had no real understanding of her role. For the observer it was reassuring to know that Tara had contact with an outsider who was aware of her home life.

Parents

Parents find it difficult to appreciate that their very dependent young child is reaching an adult age where more independent choices would be appropriate. Having taken the opportunity to send their children to Wentwood they recognised that the two year training course had *'given them their independence'*, a phrase reiterated in most interviews. In many cases they underestimated the risks taken in such training and maintained that Wentwood was situated in a sheltered village. In fact it was sited just off a busy main road in a small town and their homes were in infinitely quieter and safer areas. Most parents accepted that their children had regressed since returning home but felt unable to continue the regime.

Possibly such parents could derive support from a key worker who could work with them to foster further independence. With a parent at home and a key worker waiting at the local shops, which were near most homes, independent shopping trips could be arranged with the parents overseeing the start of the short journey and the key worker meeting client at the other end. The key worker, one of the better concepts of care in the community, seems to have failed to achieve a significant presence in the family home. If key workers do not come to the home parents should seek them out because they are able to offer support to both the client and the client's family.

As seen from the transcripts, many parents talked about, and treated, their adult sons and daughters like children. Bruce's mother did so but, unlike others, realised both the difficulties of building choices into his life and the inappropriateness of her behaviour. However difficult, parents should be aware of the growing independence of their now adult offspring and try to build some personal choices into their lives. Even over issues as small as – what time is bed time?

DISCUSSION
The Independent Group
The dictionary definition of independent is 'not depending on authority', 'unwilling to be under obligation to others'.

It would be difficult to find a group of 50 young adults who have been better trained to live a relatively independent life. Throughout the text the lives of people who are living 'independently' are explored in several chapters and it is apparent that, as the novelty wears off, they are often lonely and isolated within the local community. Where the keyworker system is in evidence people are coping well with their practical problems and working lives. For many, their emotional lives appear to be barren, social life is minimal and everybody is dependent on support staff to help them with their financial problems.

On the evidence of this sample – who speak for themselves – the concept of independent living would appear to be flawed in relation to young people with learning disabilities. Interestingly, several people living in group homes had achieved a higher level of independence and measured life skills than those who were living more independent lives in their local community.

SALIENT ISSUES

Possibly Gillian's mother (whose case study is presented in Chapter 5) articulates what many see as the salient issue of independent living. In the enthusiasm to find better lives for people with developmental disabilities, the problems of their continuing emotional dependency on 'staff' had not been fully recognised.

> Everybody thinks its better for her to get on two buses and we've fussed for her to go to work and all the rest of it, you see. But the others go to the day centres. We've fought for it, as it were, and now we're stuck with it. I remember saying quite recently why don't we listen to what Gillian is saying. Self advocacy and all that stuff. Gillian's saying that she wants to go and work at the day centre. Why can't we let her do that? Basically she's doing all the things in the community that she would be doing in the centre – with the same people when you think about it. Whether we want it now – we've got it. But now we've got it – it's a different matter.

> *She does seem to have a very full life – really she's achieved the blueprint – an ordinary life –*

> But whether the blueprint is what we really want we'll never know. Who drew up the blueprint?

CHAPTER 3

The Workers

At the time of the research 52 per cent of the ex-students, aged between 24 and 28 were involved in full and part time work or work-experience. A further 10 per cent had held similar jobs which they had had to leave due to such external factors as change of location or the offer of further education opportunities. Ten per cent were still completing further education courses and were expecting to go on government Youth Training Schemes (YTS) or find job placements. This suggested that at least 72 per cent of the cohort were capable of holding jobs and, in the event of work being available, would probably be in a position to make a realistic choice between working with their more able peers or availing themselves of whatever sheltered occupation was provided in their locality. All the ex-students (whether working or not) had attended Further Education courses for students with special needs in their local colleges and had enjoyed completing the various specially designed City and Guild type practical courses.

As part of the Wentwood curriculum the Wentwood ex-students had completed work-experience placements in local shops and institutions. Many had also lived in local lodgings for a short time and been responsible for paying their own weekly rent. This experience was intended to prepare them for the discipline of getting themselves up in the mornings and travelling to work each day. Interviews with ex-students and parents indicated that without such specific training this work ethos would not have been internalised to become part of each person's expectation of adult daily life.

The following excerpt from interviews with some of the workers highlight their comparative independence and job satisfaction, contrasted with their total inability to comprehend the financial aspects of their employment or everyday life. The problems illustrated are common to all the workers. Other aspects of their lives are looked at in other chapters. The ethics of the financial arrangements are beyond the scope of this research but where the workers lived at home an indication of the feelings of the families involved are presented in this chapter.

Lily
Lily, aged 24, lives in a flat for four people within a MENCAP group home scheme and was rated as being independent. She worked every day and was

unique in being the only person who was aware of how much she was paid. She left Wentwood with a final score of five out of six for 'money' and a nil score for 'time'. She retained some of her money skills and now had a full six score for 'time'. However, later in the interview when talking about shopping she showed very little idea of the value of money. She obtained four out of six skills in the final Wentwood mobility section which had now increased to five.

Work

Where do you work? At— [names a large store] and I do cleaning two hours I do. *Do they pay you?* Yes. *How do you get the money?* On Saturday after I finished work. I have to be there at 8 o'clock – I get up at six.

How? Its very easy. *Have you got an alarm clock?* Yes and the night staff wake us up in the morning – the two people going to work. *What would happen if they didn't – or forgot, would you wake up?* Yes I go out at 7.40 and I walk there for 8 o'clock. *What do you wear for work?* Trousers and I change when I come back.

How did you learn to do the work? I did it. *Did they tell you when you first went?* No. *You had to do it – how did you find out what to do?* I just did it, it's a shop, you clean the shop. *You knew how to clean?* Yes I do. *Is there anyone else there so early?* No only me. *Well who opens it up?* Debbie; she works there. *Does she clean too?* No she works there. *Do you have to wait till she comes?* No she comes at half past seven.

Do you have a coffee when you're working? Yes. *Who makes it?* I do. *Does Debbie talk to you while you work?* Yes we do a lot of talking. *You know you go to work at eight and you finish at what time?* 10 o'clock. *How long do you work for?* Two hours.

Money

How much money do you get at work? £15 – *money or a cheque?* No – money. *What do you do with it?* I bring it back here and keep it in my tin. *Is that your own money?* Yes.

When you go shopping do you know how much change you need? No. *If you're spending 80p do you know how much you get back from £1?* No – it's mine.

Yes it's your money and when you go to Boots and you have to buy your shampoo – how much is your shampoo – do you know? No. *How do you know how much money to give them?* I give them pounds and they give me change. *When you go and buy your shampoo how much money do you give them?* £2.

And they give you change back because you can't work the change out? Yes. *If I wrote this down in money how much money would I want?* £1.50. *That's right – but how much money would you give me?* [long pause] £1.50? *Yes but what is £1.50* – I don't know.

Do you go to the bank with your money? I've been and come back to Abbey National and the Woolwich. *Do you keep it yourself?* Mum keeps two books and I have my book here. I've got my Abbey National here – *and do you put your £12 in?* £15, yes. *Do you take it out?* Yes. *Does mum go with you?* No only me.

Ada

Ada, aged 28, still lived at home and had left Wentwood with a final score of two out of six for 'money' and a nil score for 'time'. it is doubtful whether she had retained any money skills but had increased her time score by one. Her final mobility score was four out of six which she had now increased to five. Registered partially sighted, she took a taxi to work but managed to go by bus into town to do voluntary work at Oxfam.

Work

What do you like doing best? Going to P—. *What do you do there?* Clean the bathrooms and things. *Oh you work?* Yes – *you didn't tell me you work, you work at P—?* Yes. *That's a hotel isn't it?* Yes. *What day do you go?* Tuesday and Fridays – *you like cleaning best?* Yes – *and how do you get to work?* I gets a taxi. *Who pays for it?* My mum does.

How long have you been there? Quite a while now. *What do you wear when you clean, you look very smart now?* A blue overall, skirt and a blouse. *Do they pay you?* Yes, *How?* A cheque. *When do you get the cheque?* Every month? *How much is it?* I don't know. *What do you do with it?* Sometimes I keep it. *How do you turn it into money?* My mum pays it in. *How much do you get a week?* I don't know.

Would you like to work more than the two days or is that enough? That's enough. *Do you get very tired?* Yes. *What time do you start work?* 9 o'clock I start. *What time do you finish?* 4 o'clock. *That's a long day* – I know, I gets very tired – I go to sleep in the end – *where?* Here when I get home. *Did you work yesterday?* Yes. *What did you do?* Do the bedrooms and that – *do people leave the bedrooms very dirty?* Yes. *What do they leave?* Rubbish in the bins and that.

Does the taxi come and collect you or do you phone when you want it? Mum rings the taxi up and I wait for it. *How much does the taxi cost?* £1.80 – *that's not bad* – No. *Have you got any friends at work?* I talk to someone – *but they're not friends* – No.

MOTHER

What does she get in wages?

£60. We've got to be a bit careful because of her pension. Now I think she earns just over the limit of what she should earn but nobody said anything – I can't remember how much it is they're allowed to earn a week.

How do you feel about this because she works very hard – and doesn't earn very much?

No but there's two ways of looking at this – even if she had a job where she was working part time every day, she wouldn't get as much money doing that as what she gets through her income support and pension and I feel she would lose out if she didn't have as much money.

She doesn't do as many rooms as the others do. She does about six and I think they've got about 18 to do. So that's fair in a way. She couldn't get through that many. They did give her an extra day but after about a month they said she couldn't cope with it –

She said she's very tired when she's finished –

She used to be when she first started, then she would sleep all the time – I thought it was a bit too much for her because she's got a congenital heart but then she got used to it.

How did she learn to do it the beginning?

She went with a lady who showed her then she gradually did it on her own – I can't really remember, she's been there a couple of years now.

So she's kept the job?

Yes sometimes she comes home and says 'they tell me I've got to be quicker' or I haven't done so and so today – 'I had to go back because I didn't clean the toilets today'.

Do you ever ask how she's doing?

I haven't been in touch with them because they tend to get in touch with Yvonne [key-worker]. She said they were quite pleased with her.

Money
ADA

Don't you get lonely by yourself? Yes sometimes. *What do you do when you're lonely?* Not a lot. *What would you like to do?* Go to the cinema and that. *Can't you do that on your own?* Don't do it on my own, it's difficult to buy the ticket. *Is it?* Yes. *Why?* I don't know. *Is there anything you'd like to do that you can't do?* I'd like to do sums and that. *Sums?* Yes – *didn't you do that at the centre?* No, no.

Why do you want to do sums. I find sums very difficult don't you? Do you – *yes, what sort of sums do want to do?* Money sums, I can't do that very well. *What do you do when you've got to pay money to buy your blouse in Oxfam?* I choosed it by myself. *Who paid for it?* I did.

How did you know how much money to give? £2.99. *What did you give them?* Pound coins – *oh right – if you've got to do anything do you just give pound coins?* Yes – *and then you get the change. Do you know if you get the right change?* I'm not quite sure. *If its £2.99 and you gave £3 how much money would you get back – can you remember what they gave you back?* No.

What do you do with the cheques? I don't know; mum pays it in to the bank. *Do you keep your book?* No. *Do you see your book?* No.

MOTHER

How does she get her money? Usually on a Monday I give her £10 and that's got to last her the week – *and what happens on Tuesday* – extra to that she has her taxi fares. *She says you pay that?*

I give her the money to pay it and if she comes home and she's seen something she likes in town I give her more money.

How much does she actually go through in a week?

She'd go through a lot if you would let her but I try and give her the £10 and say you've got to make that last for the week and then when I find out it's all gone by Wednesday I want to know what she's done with it – she's usually bought six pairs of knickers – or some thing that she doesn't really need – she's gone and bought them because she's seen them and she likes them.

She doesn't have her savings book. Have you ever thought of letting her have it and try to show her what the money was worth? Where does her pension go?

I have it and all her money is kept away and whatever she wants is taken out of that. I get an attendance allowance for her, I didn't even know I was entitled to it. I only have the day one. I didn't have it where we lived before. I was told I couldn't get anything for her and then my husband was told at work that we should put in for it but I was always told we'd never get it. But we did put in for it and we got it.

She's not very good with money – she likes to spend it – if you give her £10 it doesn't mean any more to her than £5. If she wants something in town she'll come home and say its £2.99 when its £10.99. If she's been in town and sees something she likes and asks if she can have it I give her the money.

How do you know how much it costs? She usually says something like its £5.99 so I give her £10. *So if it's more than £10 she can't buy it?* That's right!

Jane

Jane, aged 24, still lived at home in a rural area ill served by public transport. She had left Wentwood with a final score of two out of six for 'money' and a nil score for 'time'. She had not retained her money skills nor increased her time score. Her final mobility score had been three out of six which had now decreased to two through lack of practice.

Work

> *How do you get to work?* Mummy takes me. *Every day?* Yes. *Do you work every day?* Yes, with Wednesday off for cooking. *Where do you do cooking?* College. *How do you get there?* Mummy takes me and taxi back. *Do you do any cooking for yourself here?* Cooking NO! I make tinned shepherds pie!

> *What do you do at work?* I do all sorts, sometimes I strip wires. *Is it an electrical firm?* Yes, *How do you strip wires?* With a wire stripper. *Do you ever cut the ends by mistake?* No. *What else do you do?* What else do I do – sending jobs out – do them and send them.

> (MUM: Didn't you put lights in life jackets, what did you used to do with them?)

> We don't do them any more they glue them now. We put short wires and a long wire and solder them in.

> *How did you learn to do it – who showed you?* Who showed us – Brian – *did you find it hard?* No not really. *Did you make any mistakes?* No *How long have you been there?* Don't know.

> (DAD: Ever since she left Wentwood, five years.)

> *If you are unhappy at work who do you tell?* No-one – *don't you tell mum?* No *What do you do?* Keep working!

> DAD: This is the biggest problem ever – she learned how to use public transport at Wentwood and she's never been able to really use it here because there isn't any public transport as such here that gets anywhere where she wants to be. She can't get to work by public transport – it's ten minutes by car.

> MUM: It works out OK 'cause Mondays I don't work, Tuesdays I only work in the morning so I can pick her up – Thursday she has lunch at home with us and then we take her back to work in the car. This is the drawback – we spend most of our lives taking Jane to work and back.

> DAD: I come back for lunch every day because I work very near here. Jane virtually spends Wednesday on her own here. I pick her up about 4 o'clock and take her to college.

Money

JANE

> *Do they pay you?* Yes wage slip. *You get a wage slip.* Yes, sure. *You get a wage slip and real money?* Yes. *Real money not a cheque?* Not a cheque, real money,

but they don't do it no more. *How much do they give you?* How much do they give me? I don't know.

(MUM: she's no idea about money, £50 a week)

Does she get a pension?

MUM: No she doesn't get any benefit money. Before she had the last rise I phoned to see if she was eligible for income support – it was about £1 a week it was hardly worth going to all the rigmarole. She certainly wouldn't be eligible for it now. There are times when they have no work or they're very short of work. She's laid off. So I said if she doesn't work – don't pay her, but they said she should be.

DAD: It's a funny old thing really because she's never been in the system really apart from when she was at Wentwood. I was just getting the defence up for the poll tax. I was really getting fired up over that. We had a bit of a rigmarole because she didn't have a benefit book or anything like this and they wouldn't accept her situation. I had to get her a medical certificate in the end to get her exempt from poll tax – I was really getting charged up. If we were to charge her a rent for living at home her income would be nil – nothing – so what are you going to do about it? We didn't get that far, in the end they agreed.

That's what happens in this country today – the more you put yourself out to try and help yourself the more you'll miss out on benefits and it's really the wrong way round. The thing that always baffles me is when you hear about how much it actually costs to keep somebody in an institution. When they're talking thousands of pounds per head per month and yet when you have somebody at home you get no support at all.

Do you ever buy yourself anything with money? No.

MUM: She never spends any money. She never seems to buy anything for herself.

Tom

Tom, aged 28, lived in a group home and had left Wentwood with a final score of six out of six for 'money' and one out of six for 'time'. He had retained no money skills but had increased his time score by one. His final mobility score had been four out of six which he had now increased to five.

Work

What do you do all week – do you go to the centre? No. *Where do you go?* McDonalds three days. Mondays till 1 o'clock, Tuesday just up to 3 o'clock and Wednesday 9–1 o'clock *– and what do you do there –* work. *How long have* *you been going?* Since 1991. *How do you get there?* I always go by bus from here to town.

Do you have your dinner there? Yes. *What do you have?* Large chips, chicken in a bun, large diet coke and a chocolate doughnut. *Every day?* Yes. *You're very thin for all that food, is it good food?* Yes.

HOUSE MANAGER: Did you explain about what you did on Wednesday. You do different things on Wednesday, you have a big delivery into McDonalds and you unload it. He goes to staff meetings each Monday. I think you personally do well to travel independently don't you Tom?

Do you go to staff meetings? Yes, staff meetings with the – manager – store manager, June and the cleaning supervisor.

Money
MOTHER

I couldn't imagine two or three boys together without staff – how could they manage money and shopping. I always think about that – these kids having money – and he will go into a pub to have a drink. To a certain extent he understands the money but I don't think he understands the change. He knows the price of this and the price of that and the price of the other.

Do you think he's capable of handling his own pension?

I don't think so, he never seems to know about things like that and I do ask him. When he lived here he had the allowance from the DHSS and he had that money and he kept that himself.

Could you send him shopping on his own?

Yes, little bits – go to the bank and pay a bill, he could do that but I gave him the right money.

Colin
Colin, aged 23, lived in a group home and left Wentwood with a final score of six out of six for 'money' and a nil score for 'time'. He had retained no money skills but had increased his time score by one. His final mobility score was four out of six which he had now increased to five. He travelled independently to work at the local Co-op and called in at his home each day on his way back from work before returning to the group home.

Work

What do you do at work? I do fruit and vegetables.

What do you do with them?

> Well we do the apples in the box, empty the box and after that put new ones in, and then put the old ones back in again as well so we can take the old apples in the box.

Oh so you sell the old apples first? Yes. *How much are they?* [long silence] *Can't you remember?* 24p. *What sort of apples are they?* They're golden delicious. *What time do you catch the bus to work?* 8 o'clock *and what time do you catch it home?* 3 o'clock.

Do you work every day? I work Monday Tuesday, Thursday and Friday. *What do you do Wednesday?* Wednesday my day home. *How did you get your job?* Mr T interviewed me. *Do they pay you?* No. *You just do it voluntarily?* Yes. *Where do you get your money from?* I get my money from the Post Office and the green card.

If you didn't work what would you do? [long pause] Do work experience. *Is this work experience?* Yes.

> MOTHER: This job he has now he had it during the YTS and he was also at Woolworths YT but they wouldn't keep him on to do voluntary work. He's in the Co-op now and he's on the fruit department. They rotate, it's a supermarket so he doesn't have to sell. He talks to the customers and he's right by the doorway and several times he's come and there have been elderly people and he's gone round with them pushing their trolleys and getting their shopping for them. He's very competent and he can read. He was two years at college doing academic work and two years doing YTS. This work he has now was his YTS placement but they kept him on. MENCAP are trying to find him a job. They may give him a paid job at the Co-op but its all problems with the money and what have you.

Money
MOTHER

> He will not carry money if he can help it. He gets himself a paper every day and he has the right money exactly now. If he's going to the shops to get his paper and the TV times every week he likes to take a pound so that they will give him the change or a £5 note or a £10 note.

Has he any idea what the change should be?

> I don't know but they overcharged him down at the shop and he said no that's not right!

COLIN

What do you do about money? Staff give it. *How much do you get?* I don't know because I have my lunch money. I have 59p for lunch. *Have you got a Post Office book?* Yes. *Who keeps it?* I do. *Do you put money in and take money out?* Yes. *Where do you keep your money?* I keep my money in my bedroom.

How much is a pint of beer down here?

It's... [long silence]... You take a fiver with you and you give it to the barman and then after that the barman gives you more money.

When you want the next beer – another beer – what do you do? I give the money to him – *which money...* [silence] – *the money that's left from the fiver?* Yes – *and he gives you more money back?* Yes.

Do you find it difficult trying to find out how much things cost – how much money to give? No.

What do you do if you go into town shopping. What do you give them? A fiver. *Always?* Yes – *and get change back* – yes. *Do you get a receipt?* Yes. *What do you do with the receipt?* Put it in my pocket and give it to the staff.

HOUSE MANAGER: We have a problem with money. One day a week he has a home day and he will go shopping and he'll have to go and buy his food for the day. Now he will go out and we give him two or three pounds out of petty cash. He decides what he'd like to buy before he goes. He goes on his own obviously. He comes back – he has absolutely no idea of the change and will usually argue about the amount. He'll mix his own money up with the money that has been given to him. This happens every time.

He has his green sheet. Say for instance he wanted to buy a present for mum's birthday and he'd want to buy a tape. We'd say that's about £9 isn't it and he would then have his money off the sheet. Its absolutely open, he can see always see it. Obviously we would never show anyone any other client's. There's often not a great deal of money on it. We work differently with each client according to their needs because we feel it's not fair if they can't handle their money. We feel if they're not able then we gradually initiate them and they have more to do with their own money. It may be that they are never going to be able to.

Mark

Mark, aged 27, lived in a flat in a MENCAP group home and still returned home every weekend. He had left Wentwood with a nil final score for 'money' and a nil score for 'time', neither of which he had increased. His final mobility score was three out of six which had now decreased to two. He travels independently to work.

Work

What do you do at McDonalds? I clear all the tables – *and what else do you do?* Help the customers. *Do you wipe the tables?* I wipe the tables yes and put things in bins. *You like that?* I like that – I go by bus – just one bus. *If you're unhappy at work and something goes wrong who do you turn to?* My boss.

MOTHER: McDonalds have been extremely good – I couldn't really praise them enough the kindness and courtesy they've given to Mark. He's now taking a three day course at the college and they've adapted his hours – he's there from 10 o'clock to 4 o'clock. It's more or less their attempt to normalise relationships between mentally handicapped youngsters and the community. He's got his three City and Guild certificates – its a specially adapted course with a certificate from London.

Money

What do you do about money? I go to the bank. *How do you get the money?* Staff gets it. *Do you keep any money?* It's kept in the office, sometimes in my room. *If you want money to go out what do you do?* Ask the staff.

MOTHER: He has £5 a week pocket money and puts that in a box in his drawer and he uses a pound a day. He's supposed to go in the office for any other money he wants.

DAD: I've never met one who could understand money – he's no idea. When the old 10p pieces were discontinued he'd come home with a pocket full of 10p pieces that people had given him – he couldn't understand. I wouldn't trust him with money. When he fetches his money from the bank he just comes out holding it instead of putting it in his pocket. He can't make a phone call from a box with money. We've tried and persist in trying but not enough training is given to these youngsters because they could do such a lot more but it has to be taught on a one to one basis.

Ann and Judy

Ann and Judy are 28-year-old twins who were premature births weighing 1lb 15oz and 1lb 12oz respectively. They are attractive, charming and confident, with beautiful manners, and often speak as one person. Both are very thoughtful and show surprising insight into their condition. Good vocabulary masks deceptively poor academic skills. Both speak and think very slowly but Judy has a high pitched slightly whining voice, far from normal. Their perception of their own disability and that of their peers is explored in Chapter 5. They live with two other similarly disabled people in a supported house run by a housing association who are the largest provider of accommodation for people with developmental disabilities in the area. The house is in the centre of town. Their reliance on the minimal support given by their key worker for all their financial dealings suggests that fully independent living will not be a realistic option for either of them.

They were the two most able Wentwood ex-students and had both left Wentwood with a final scores of six out of six for mobility. Ann scored one and Judy four on 'time'. Ann had now reached Judy's 4 score and Judy had not increased her time score. Judy had a final money score of six and Ann five. Neither had changed. Their IQs had been estimated at various times as below IQ50 and they had both been to special schools.

Work

What else do you do Ann – do you work? Yes, I go to a cafe twice a week. *When do you go?* One to five Monday and Friday. *How did you get that job?* It was through Bill wasn't it? *Is he a social worker?* No. Key worker.

Where did you meet him? In skills and opportunities. *Is he attached to the college?* I don't know, he just finds out about jobs. *How long have you had the job?* I don't know – is it two years or three years? I can't remember.

What do you do, Judy? I work at the Park Hotel doing the cleaning – I do one morning. I did do it more until I'm helping at the playgroup one morning. *Are you?* So I do that on Wednesdays. *How did you get that job?* I got that because I was interested in helping other people and I do another playgroup because I really like helping the children. *Did you do that at Wentwood?* Yes I did, I helped with a playgroup there.

ANN: I did that as well, I remember I have done a playgroup at Branchly. *Why did you stop?* They had enough helpers. *Were you sorry you couldn't go any more?* Yes.

JUDY: I usually walk everywhere, I like walking because it's exercise. *Mrs Reynolds made you all walk didn't she?*

I quite enjoy walking anyway. I walk to work – I enjoy it. I sometimes think I'm going to be late but if I'm a few minutes late they'll understand because its a long walk to work.

Did you have a nice birthday? Yes thank you. *What did you do?*

You were working weren't you Ann? I was working in the morning at the handicapped playgroup. In the summer I help with the handicapped childrens' holidays – I help out – its a holiday playgroup.

How old are they? About five to about eleven years old. I've been helping at it for about eight or nine years.

Money

Where do you get your money from? We have a pension. *Do you keep your own bank books?* Yes we do. *Do you keep all your own money?* Yes we've got a savings book. *Do you go and put it in yourselves?* Yes we do.

You keep all your own accounts? I keep some of it. We aren't very good at money – we're getting better. We can't do change.

Do you think people who perhaps think slowly and have difficulty with money – you say you've got difficulty with money – do you think that's a problem or not? If it's a lot of money we need help.

Is there anything you'd like to do that you can't? Filling in forms. *You find that difficult do you?* Yes complicated forms, both of us find it difficult.

[Sylvie, their support worker joined the conversation towards the end.]

What would you miss most if Sylvie wasn't here? I think someone to talk to with our problems – and money.

SYLVIE They know how much things cost and they have quite a good sense of value, but its very very hard to work out if change is right. If the receipt is there and you go to Safeways and it says the total at the end is £8.50 and you gave a £10 note and the change is £1.50. They're perfectly capable of checking to see they've got £1.50 but if that wasn't written there you couldn't work out quickly enough that £1.50 is the change you should be receiving. [Twins in unison **NO!**] So that when they just go into a cafe you have to hand over money and you don't always get a receipt, or your receipt just says what you spent. It's impossible for the ladies to check their change because they are not quick enough. I said to them to try and and have a rough idea of whether or not you should have a £5 note in your change – if you hand over £10 and you've just spent £1 you should get a £5 note or a very generous handful of pound coins. I try and eliminate the differences you can have.

If you went somewhere different and Sylvie didn't come – what would you miss most? **How to do money and forms.**

Everything we talk about, we come back to money and forms –it seems to be an enormous problem?

[Twins in unison and with emphasis.] **It is if you've got something complicated and you don't know how to do it.**

SYLVIE: And of course no sooner do we get to grips with the banking system and they change it and then it takes us a long while to get back into it.

If you have to buy some thing for 60p what do you do Ann?

ANN: **If I can make the 60p up with the right change I'd give the 60p. If it was more than that I'd give the pound. Like yesterday I went down to the card shop and I didn't have enough change to pay for the the card so I had to use one of my £5 notes.**

SYLVIE: Had you already counted your change to see? **Yes.**

JUDY: **You always come on Monday evening to check the change.**

SYLVIE: You can't check your food money by yourself, that's the problem but you can do all the other things. They know how much money to put in each pot.

Sylvie if you were ill and didn't come – you must be ill sometimes – what would happen? The hours are so limited I can usually work round it.

Trevor

Trevor, aged 20, lived at home and had left Wentwood with a nil final score for 'money' which he had increased to two and a score of two for 'time' which he now increased to six. His final mobility score was four out of six which he had now increased to five. He worked full time for a national television station. He had the most appalling stammer which must render him effectively mute in most social situations. Although the stammer is mentioned in the Wentwood records it was obviously less severe at that time and he was well able to benefit from the curriculum and the active social life he led. He had just started speech therapy again after a lapse of a year.

Work

MOTHER   He worked in the old people's home when he left Wentwood He worked there for a year. When he left Wentwood we wouldn't send him to the ATC and the social worker came to see him and said there was a work experience job at the old people's home so they sent him there. He worked there for a year. He got on so well that he didn't want to leave but they offered him the job at TV. He'd always said he'd like to visit the TV studio since he'd been little – but even then he didn't want to leave the old people's home – but now he's there he don't want to leave there now. He wouldn't be where he is now if it weren't for Wentwood. No way.

He did a year's YTS there and they were so pleased with him that they phoned me up to say that they were so pleased with him but they didn't think they could keep him on as TV's money was low. If they could get a sponsorship they'd take him on. They got the sponsorship. They said they'd never seen the kitchens so clean. He does the kitchens – wipes all the tables down.

What does he do about the bus to work?

> He's got a bus pass. When he started first we had to write it on a piece of paper – it's his stammer – that's what I think it is.

How does he get on at work?

> I asked them a couple of times and they said he just gets on with his work. They say 'Good morning Trevor – how did you get on at the weekend' but he has a job to answer because of his stammer and everything – it makes it very difficult for him.

[Trevor comes in. Clearly he finds it difficult to answer but by making sure there was no hurry he managed to stammer out the answers. Although transcribed as coherent script it took a long time to elicit the information. Once he had actually managed to start a sentence he seemed to have little difficulty completing it.]

You look very smart, are those your working clothes?

> MUM: No, he's got a uniform – he's got blue trousers – a white shirt and a blue and white waistcoat and a white hat. I buy his clothes, he says he don't want new clothes – he says 'I got a jumper.' [Trevor adds **'yes'** to all this]

Do you know any of the people there, Trevor?

Trevor repeats the names of the media personalities he works with.

Do you actually see them – is the kitchen attached to the canteen? **Yes.**

Do you do any cooking? **No cleaning and clearing tables.**

Do you see the stars when you clear the tables? **Yes.**

What do you have for lunch? **Chips, fresh fruit and chilli con carne.**

What did you have for lunch today? **Pasty and chips.**

How much do you get paid? **£90.**

Do you get one bus to work or do you have to change buses? **Two buses.**

Have you ever been on a bus into town for anything else? **No.**

You just go on a bus to work in town? **Yes.**

Is there anything that you want to do that you can't do? **I want to be camera man.** *A camera man?* **Yes.** *Have you got a video camera here at home?* **Yes. I want to be a television camera man.** *Have you ever used a videocamera?* **Yes.** *Have you ever had a go of a TV camera?* **No.** *Why don't you ask – is that what you'd really like to do?* **Yes.** *Do you think you could do it?* **Yes.**

MUM: He's always said he wants to be a camera man.

Money

> MUM: At the moment we just cannot get him to understand money.

Don't you like handling money? **No.**

> MUM: On a Saturday if I haven't got my paper he'll get it and I give him the right money.

Will you buy anything else – like groceries? **No.** *Why not, is it the money?* **Yes.** *Do you smoke?* **No.**

> MUM: He puts all his money in the bank and takes a pound a day.

If it all goes in the bank, Trevor, how do you get the money out to buy things?

> MUM: He don't have money to buy things. He's always got money in his pocket. The same money's been in his pocket about three or four months. I tell him to go and buy a bar of chocolate but he will not go and get anything.

You don't spend any money at work – you've got your bus pass and get your lunch? Do you ever go to the pub? **No.**

Have you got your own bank book, Trevor?

> MUM: Yes I keep it for him.

Does he go and get it out?

> No, no we give him money if he wants money – but he don't ever want money. He gets his bus pass and his clothes and that.

Do you take anything for his keep? I just draw it out when I need it.

Who pays for your holidays? **Mum.** *How much money have you got on you now?* **Er –**

> MUM: He's always got 10p pieces on him for the phone.

Nick

Nick was a lively 25-year-old with a measured IQ of 41 and remarkably good communication skills. He was one of ten children and lived at home. In the interview money and work were treated as one subject.

After you left Wentwood you went to college for two years and then YTS and now you've got a job? **Yes, I'm a gardener.**

> MUM: He's studying horticulture it's part of YTS scheme but this time it's a proper job.

Do they pay you? **Oh yes, wages.** *Do you get it at the end of the week?* **Yes.** *How much do they pay you?* **They give me £108.**

MUM: A fortnight. He doesn't get a pension. They stopped that when he started this. I don't know what the changeover was –

Who stopped the pension? Don't ask me, somebody suggested something or other and that was it.

If you lived on your own you'd have to pay rent? **Yes.**

MUM: They would pay it then, but because he's living at home – no. It's all right looking after your children until they're grown up but when they get to a certain age you'd think they'd arrange something or other. If they go and live in a home it costs the social services a heck of a lot more – it's fairly stupid. They offered him a place in a home just down the road here –

But he doesn't want to leave home? No I don't really want him to leave either.

This £54, do you give some of it to your mother? **Yes everything** – *and how much do you keep?*

MUM: He only gives me £25 and he had to try to save some for his holidays. He gets £25 but I don't give it all to him to keep – he'll spend it and he'll lose it. He's always losing things so I have to keep it and give it him as he wants. It comes here as a cheque and he takes it to the Post Office. He goes himself and gets it.

When you go to the pub how much does a coke cost? **About 60p.** *How much do you take?* **A couple of pounds – sometimes £5.**

Do you keep him to the £25? When he goes to the disco it costs him more. *What happens if he's finished it all before the end of the week?*

Well there's things he has to go without. I tell him he's not getting any of my money but he usually does. He buys records and tapes.

Do you make him stay in when the money's gone? Sometimes I loan it him till the end of the week –

Do you pay it back? **Oh yes, I'm always paying Mum back.**

If you could live at home with Mum and do all things you did at Wentwood – would you rather do that, or be where you are now? **I'd rather do the things I done at Wentwood.**

MUM: He does lot at work. He leaves here at 7.30 and doesn't get home till 6.30.

Sarah

Sarah was a thoughtful 24-year-old lady with Down's syndrome. Although not having the highest Wentwood leaving score, five years later she had developed and gained skills that gave her a post Wentwood score in advance of the entire sample. Her mother held strong views about the education and lifestyle of people with developmental disabilities and being unable to find a suitable placement that would continue the Wentwood curriculum, she started her own group home. She now administrates two such homes which are already virtually self-supporting and a third is opening shortly. Everybody works on the land and in the country craft workshops whilst also participating in continuing education, regardless of age. The residents also do all the domestic work in the house. Excerpts from an interview with a member of staff precede Sarah's interview.

Mr Smith was a local farmer with his own butcher shop who on retirement sold his business but became bored within six months and looked for 'something to be involved in'. He had no experience of any form of disability and his work training methods give a good example of those of other employers who also learned by trial and error.

Do you find it difficult dealing with people who are not very bright? Not really. *Did you have staff in your butcher's shop?* Yes. *These must be very different?*

Not really, you've just got to accept their limitations, go very slowly and prepare a lot of the work. Now if I've got girls there, I'm pricking out now, some of them are pretty good. Sarah is very good and there's a handful of girls who are really quite good in the spring at pricking out all the bedding out plants. We sold three or four hundred trays of bedding out plants. Even then there is a lot of preparatory work to do. It's very rare that they can even fill the tray and get it level so you've got to keep checking all the time. Then I put markers down the side of the tray where every row has got to be because they can't put the rows evenly down the tray.

Can they follow the rows?

Well I've got a little device that makes four holes across the tray. When I put the markers down the side of the tray they've then got a little gadget which I got made up for me that puts four holes at a time so that the rows then go across.

So they can do that?

Yes, I've got one or two who don't spend much time with me. A lot of them don't care for it all that much – it just depends who they put here. Of course the weather can be pretty nasty too but we do keep going all the time. The local garage keep a trolley down there which I keep stocking with plants and they sell them and we get the money from them.

Do you charge a competitive price?

A bit less really, especially when it comes to bedding plants and so on which might not be quite as good as they might be. You get a bit of irregularity. They tend to damage the roots when they're pricking out so you may get a tray of 24 with only 20 good plants.

Money

A member of staff joined Sarah during the next part of the interview and became quite appalled during this conversation of which only the latter half is quoted. Sarah was an independent traveller who not only shopped in the nearby city but also took herself to London on the coach. She went out for meals and shopping with friends from the group home and also appeared to be able to manage her own finances. In the light of her obvious ability, the conversation below was an eye opener to the member of staff concerned but only too predictable for the author! As the full story of Sarah's shopping trip unfolded the staff member finally became speechless.

Sarah, how much do you get on pay day? **Don't know.**

STAFF: How much do you get? **25.** 25 what? **Pounds.** Come on, you know you sign for it, you sign for what is written. **Yes, but I don't know how much.**

STAFF: You get £12.50. I personally explained this to all of you. We are given £12.65 per week for each person, 15p of that I am saving for you through the year and giving you as a bonus and we all agreed that that was a very sensible thing to do. You would be given £12.50 each week and 15p saved as a bonus through the year and when the year comes to an end they will get their bonus. Where does the money come from that's in your post office book?

SARAH: **Don't know.** What do you sometimes do on a Saturday after you've been paid? **Go to the post office?** What do you do if you want money to buy clothes? **Go to the post office.**

Sarah when you get your £12 on a Saturday how is it paid? What does it look like? [silence] *er. You've bought it with you today haven't you?* **Yes.** *What sort of money have you brought with you today?* **Pound notes.** *How many?* **One £5.** *Look at it, what is it?* **£5.**

STAFF: It's £10. You know that's a ten pound note Sarah. [Uncertainly and plainly willing to please] **Yes.**

STAFF: They have their own cash books and we go through it every week. And so they know exactly how much, they write down how much they get. If you write it down very slowly and work it out very slowly she can actually do that and understand how much she's spent but it takes a long time. They can't do it in the shop over the counter.

Where is your cash book Sarah? **In my bedroom.** *You took your money on Saturday pay day and you went shopping – where did you go to buy your crayons?* **W H Smith.** *How much did they cost?* **About £1.50.** *Did you have your £12.50 with you?* **Yes.**

What else did you buy? **A calendar.** *How much were they?* **About £12 – and what else did you buy?** **Rubbers.** *Did you have enough money when you got to the till?* **Yes – er I had to put some back.** *Did you, what did you have to put back, what couldn't you afford to pay for?* **I couldn't afford the cassette.**

Did you put it in your basket and have to put it back? **Yes.** *When you got to the till had you spent more money than you had?*

Yes, I put back the cassette and a calender and I got left with two packs of pens and I got some change. *How much change did you get?* **About one or two.** *Little money like this, brown money?* **Yes.**

Were there a lot of people behind you when you paid? **Yes.** *Did they have to wait for you?* **Yes.** *Were they cross?* **Some were not cross – and some were cross – yes.** *What did they say?* **It doesn't matter.** *Did you have to go yourself and put them back?* **No the lady did it.**

Did you bring the receipts back? **Yes in my purse.** *Did you spend all your money?* **Yes.** *So you had to wait till next Sat for more money?* **Yes.** *Did you buy a return bus ticket when you went?* **Yes.** *So you had enough money to come home?* **Yes.**

When not struggling with her financial affairs Sarah was articulate and thoughtful. She read adult magazines and has written stories. She enjoyed her craft and garden work and, as Mr Smith pointed out, was a skilful worker. Chapter 2 gives evidence of her and philosophical approach to her own life situation and a very clear indication of the way she wishes to live. She articulated much of what the less articulate people tried to say.

DISCUSSION

The special schools people had attended before going to Wentwood had not fostered the hope that work would be the preferred option for such school leavers. Parents expressed amazement that their children had returned home at the end of the Wentwood course with not only the ability to work but the expectation that this was to be the norm. Most parents expressed pride and pleasure at this unexpected post Wentwood development and the fact that the curriculum had given their children such a positive and confident approach to work. Over and over again they said that without such intensive one-to-one training by dedicated dispassionate professionals such development would not have been possible. These views are validated by the resulting skill losses of the ex-students who returned to live at home after completing their course.

Several women with Down's Syndrome said that they found the further education courses both strenuous and tiring. They had also given up jobs and work experience placements, which were well within their capabilities because they found working life too tiring, too noisy and too rushed. Although it is beyond the scope of this research, clear evidence was found of a developmental difference with age in young adults with Down's Syndrome which was more pronounced in women than men. They clearly and succinctly expressed their discomfort within the work environment, town centres, busy supermarkets and even the adult training centre. The general literature in this field appears to be more concerned with prognosis rather than causal factors. The evidence presented by young adults with Down's syndrome in this sample suggests, quite simply, that their general hypotonic muscular development which slows down all their physical responses, combined with a slow cognitive response, superimposes a barrier between them and the fast moving environment they inhabit.

Within the group of workers it was difficult to find any homogeneity. No particular type of living environment appeared to be more favourable or more conducive to work. There was evidence that workers who lived at home in the small protective nuclear family caused more family disruption than did people who were living either in group homes or more independent provisions. However, families rearranged their lives to accommodate the worker and group homes similarly rearranged schedules to facilitate workers. Consequently there was no evidence of anyone who had a job being being hindered in any way. It was noticeable that in group homes the ex-Wentwood students were usually the only people who both had jobs and travelled independently to them. Those ex-students who had relinquished jobs had done so because they wished to. All the workers appeared to enjoy their work and were well regarded at their workplace. Several people were kept on after their work-experience placements finished and had now been in the same job for up to five years.

The only exception was one lady who had been sacked when a long term relationship had been discovered between herself and the married manager of her workplace. The female manager of her group home was so incensed by this lady's distress, exploitation, and the loss of the job which she had held for two years, that she took the case to Court and ensured that the man concerned was also sacked. The lady was very disturbed by the experience and given therapeutic help on a one-to-one basis for many months before she found a similar placement elsewhere which she still enjoys.

It seemed clear that whatever the workers were doing they were doing well and were not giving any cause for concern. Of particular interest is the fact that very few appeared to be specifically trained for whatever type of work they were doing. Many of the work experience placements had been obtained by MENCAP pathway workers or through the Colleges of Further Education, yet although these agencies were aware of the range of jobs available they only appeared to be implementing training programmes for catering and gardening. The training focussed on manual skills and there was little effective attempt to train the workers to cope with the financial side of their jobs. Money skills were taught either in the abstract or in relation to shopping.

When the ex-students were asked how they learned to do the requisite work the reply was invariably 'I just did it'. When asked how they knew what to do – 'I did.' This exchange was repeated with the majority of the workers. It appeared that knowing little about disability, employers treated the ex-students like any other employee; and like everybody else they just learned! A similar situation was reported in Sinson (1993) where older institutionalised patients of a mental subnormality hospital were relocated to a group home. They found work in the local village with few problems. The local publican who had formerly worked in mental handicap saw no need to treat the handicapped employee much different from the other workers. The teacher trained in special needs, who now ran the market garden, got an acceptable performance from her employees without resorting to the special training she was well qualified to do.

The list of employers and range of jobs held by the workers is impressive. Kodak, McDonalds, Argos, The Co-op, Marriott and other hotels, gardening jobs, homes for the aged, cafe's, National TV, egg packing and grading. The most surprising was a young lady working in a small electronics firm doing a variety of short contracts involving wiring objects as diverse as life-jackets and radios. With the exception of one IQ below 30 the majority of these workers had an IQ range of 30–45. Two people had severe communication difficulties and were virtually mute; the majority had a range of communication problems including severe stammering. Several of the people with Down's syndrome had almost indecipherable speech. Despite these handicaps the majority had evolved acceptable ways of communicating although, for some, social conversation was not one of their stronger points.

Although the majority of the sample had communication problems an interpreter was needed for only one person but even she, at the end of a full day, finally managed to nod or shake her head in the appropriate places. To eliminate the chance of error all information was checked back with either parents or staff and the accuracy of the information given by the working group was impressive. They were able to describe a surprising range of employments. The workers could give a detailed description of their route to work and times of their various rest breaks. They could describe their routine and the jobs for which they were responsible. Those who were employed at MacDonalds also attended the weekly staff meeting and were aware of the hierarchy of the establishment. Of those that were paid, few had any idea of how much they earned or the hourly rate for the work. Several worked two or three days and were not paid because the rate for the job was too high and would affect their pension. People who received a full weekly wage were financially worse off than those that did not. Workers in group homes were unable to accept full wages as it would invalidate their board and lodging allowance.

SALIENT ISSUES
The relationship of independent travel skills to work opportunities
The only common denominator for the majority of this group was a mobility sub-score in excess of three skills. The practical implication of this was that they were capable of independent travel and were easily trained on the journeys necessary for work which often involved either two buses or walking some way into a town to catch a bus. One of the women took a taxi to work, because there was no bus to the large hotel on the outskirts of the town where she was employed as a cleaner two days a week. However, although registered partially sighted she managed to catch a bus into town the other days of the week to do her voluntary work at Oxfam. Another lady who lived in a rural area was given lifts to and from work by her parents as there was no public transport available. Parents and staff were confident that all the workers would be well able to cope with altered travel arrangements in an emergency.

There was evidence that the emphasis in the Wentwood curriculum on training in travel (on foot, bike, bus and train) was responsible for this advantage in later life. Parents were quite clear that they would have never allowed their children to travel on their own without this training. Group homes did not have the staff nor the time to carry out the intensive Wentwood one-to-one type training. However, there was clear evidence that if the person was already an experienced traveller, staff would spend time rehearsing the journey to work until people felt confident to go by themselves.

This group of workers had no superior academic nor physical ability compared to the rest of ex-students. They had left Wentwood with very little concept of money, and often appeared to have lost most of whatever understanding they had had in this area. They had also left Wentwood with even less recorded ability to tell the time and understand the passage of time, than they had of understanding money. In many cases a nil score was recorded on the final Wentwood assessment for 'time'. Yet the ex-students who worked made considerable gains in this area and were able to achieve skills on the post-Wentwood 'time' assessment not shown by the non-workers. The need to set the alarm clock to get up for work, to go and to return from work at a specific time, catch the right numbered bus at the right time and not miss the coffee, lunch or tea break, appeared to concentrate the mind remarkably well!

Money

One of the standard questions asked towards the end of every interview was whether there was anything that the person wanted to do but couldn't – or anything that staff or family wouldn't let them do. It was anticipated that the answers would range from going to Disney Land to meeting their favourite pop-star. It was also designed to give people in group homes an opportunity to cite any restrictive practices that affected their lives.

With what became an almost predictable response from workers and non-workers alike, people cited their inability to handle money and in particular 'change' and said how foolish they felt about it when they went out. It became clear that in this particular area they had adequate insight to realise their limitations.

Parallelled with this finding was the fact that every ex-Wentwood student had been extensively taught about money in the curriculum, working from their own personal base line achievement. Teaching had also continued during the two or three years spent in further education. After leaving college, as shown in the text, many were still being helped by dedicated key-workers, group home staff and families. Most people were well taught according to the current curriculum content. It does not seem unreasonable to suggest that the method of teaching time, number and money should be reassessed in the light of the inability of school leavers to retain the information.

CHAPTER 4

Alienation

As the research progressed a totally unexpected finding regarding 20 per cent of the sample slowly emerged. These people preferred to have absolutely no contact with their similarly disabled peer group. Regardless of whatever euphemistic re-labelling has been substituted in preparation for the Care in the Community Act, in the same way that the community as such recognises that sector that is developmentally different, a group within this research sample were aware of the differences between themselves and those peers that they would *prefer* to mix with. This alienation has involved those closest to them, who help plan their lives, a fair amount of sorrow and heart searching. Parents, experienced residential staff, key-workers and the ex-students indicated their feelings about this alienation and the examples in this chapter are representative of most views.

The interviews did not include any set questions about the ex-students' perceptions of their own disability because it was felt that it could well be too emotive a subject to approach in the context of a single interview with no opportunity for a follow up. Everybody was aware that the reason they were taking part in the research was because they had been to Wentwood, and that only people who had been to Wentwood were involved. Where it seemed appropriate, and initiated by the ex-student in answer to a different question, perceptions of their own disability were explored.

An untrained manager of a private religious home, where the quality of care was outstandingly high, discussed the two ex-students in her group home who were well settled and had formed good relationships with the other residents. Jane had already had a disastrous relationship with a married man and was happy in a relationship with one of the residents.

How aware are the of residents of their handicap?

> I would say that some of them are very aware and they will tell me they're handicapped. Jane won't tell me – I know she recognises she is – don't think she doesn't – but she never talks about it. Others talk about it. David – he knows about the rejection because of the way he is but he doesn't mind being the way he is. I give him the idea that he's a very special person and his hang-ups aren't the same as ours and he lives a better life in one way because of it.

105

You meet this head on do you?

> Oh yes, I never ignore it. I never lie to them. I've never lied to anybody. If you ask me a question it's answered. They know that they'll be getting the truth – they know it won't be something off the cuff. I spend time listening – its so important to listen to what they're actually saying. Not to what they are saying *but to what they are actually saying* – there's always an element of something else that they come out with. Worries – you find that what they are actually saying is not what they're meaning – that's quite hard to guess, what's really causing that problem – it can take hours. I've learnt through 20 years of being with them. I don't believe in coddling them and I don't really believe you need a fully trained staff. There are so many people not getting to the core of the problem – I would like to make people more self-aware. Jane is equal to me – I see that very much and very clearly. At the end of the day we've all got the same needs. Some of the needs Jane has got are very special.

A highly qualified manager of similar experience in the Home Farm Trust also had two ex-students as residents who were well settled and enjoyed good relationships with the other residents. Although she felt that the most able were the most problematic this was not found in this particular research sample, but many of her residents were much older than the two ex-students.

> The unhappiest are the most able – I think they have the ability to realise their disability and I don't think they fit in anywhere. We ask them here 'Well why do you think you live here' – 'Well I'm a Down's' – 'Well why does everybody else live here – like so-and-so' 'well they're stupid'. In other words – 'I live here but I don't want to identify with them.' They don't fit in – and they don't fit in to a normal world either. This isn't ideal for them but the community isn't ideal. There must be something in the middle.

Ann and Judy, twins aged 28, were more articulate than many and although both engaged to young men with learning disabilities of similar or rather less ability than themselves, they still made a strong and clear distinction between themselves and their handicapped peers. They lived semi-independent lives in a shared house with two other learning disabled ladies whom they did not like very much and complained about the constant arguments between these other two. During the interview they often spoke in unison, for each other, or echoed each other's views. They are only differentiated in the text where each was clearly speaking for herself. Their excellent communication skills mask their lack of ability.

Do you go to the a Gateway club or anything? NO WE DON'T GO TO ANYTHING LIKE THAT [in unison and with emphasis].

You don't go anywhere where there are other people who are disabled – except college? NO – *Its only a question I have to ask!* WE DON'T GO TO ANY OF THOSE THINGS [in unison – still with emphasis].

Do you have any friends? (ANN:) I go out with my boyfriend, (JUDY:) and I go out with my boyfriend. *How long have you have had your boyfriend* (JUDY:) I've been going out with him for about eight years. *The one you met at college?* Yes.

Did you go to a school for people with learning difficulties? Yes we went to the special school.

Was that nice?

(ANN:) Yes very nice – that's why I like helping the handicapped children – I can understand that sometimes they are different because they're handicapped – I feel that sometimes they might have problems over it when they're older – you know.

What sort of problems? (ANN:) Some people may not be very nice. *Why?* I've come across that. *Have you?* When I was at school you know – *which school?* – at special school some people weren't very nice.

Where, in the special school? Yes. *Did people have handicaps at the special school?* Yes. *Do you think it's important to help people who have difficulties?* Oh yes.

How about you Judy, do you think they have problems or not?

When I worked in summer scheme some of them were in wheelchairs and they could get out of their chairs but it's just the limit of what they can do.

At Wentwood some people were there who were very slow and didn't speak very well – did you notice that or not?

I tried to help explain something to some one who was very slow but it's difficult because sometimes they can't speak.

You went from a special school to Wentwood where there were also people having problems – would you have liked to go somewhere were people didn't have so many problems – or were you quite happy? I was quite happy.

Did you think you were perhaps cleverer than the others? Um – it helped us become independent – *you mean because they taught you things?* Yes.

To go back to these people with problems – do you see yourself as having problems? Yes sometimes we can't understand things. *Do you get angry about things like that?* No we're trying hard to do things like that. *Is that why Wentwood was good?* Yes we never stopped learning there. *How do you feel Judy, do you think you've got problems or not?* I like helping other people.

Is there anything you'd like to do that you can't? We'd like to meet more people about my own age – it's very difficult.

Judy Do you feel you want to meet more people of your own age or are you quite happy? I'm quite happy.

(ANN:)   She's quite quiet and I don't meet people at work because I do sort of cleaning. My work is as hard as Judy's and anyone else's.

I'm sure it is. Do you find you don't meet many people apart from your boyfriend? Not many – *but you've both got boyfriends and you do everything with them – there's no time for anything else.*

I was at college and I didn't have a boyfriend for a long time and I can understand that it's lonely.

What sort of place do you want to live in? Maybe a flat or a house. *Do you want to live only on your own?* No with my boyfriend.

I know, but the two of you don't want to live with other people? No. *You wouldn't like to share a house with two other learning disabled people like here?*

No, I've come a long way.

Trevor

Trevor, aged 20, was tall, dark and very good looking, lived the life of a recluse and worked full time in a canteen where he was well thought of. He only left home to go to work. He was cosseted by his family who did everything for him and had no social contacts other than the family. He refused to take advantage of the many social activities available to people with learning disabilities within the city. There was some suggestion that his loneliness was leading him to make inappropriate advances to women when travelling on the bus.

MUM: Trevor would never have gone outside the door if it weren't for Wentwood. He would go out the back to play – just for a time – the kids used to make fun of him or beat him up. Trevor couldn't stand up for him himself so from then we didn't let him go outside – he just stayed in – went to school and back on the bus. When he went to Wentwood he went horse riding – went to church – he got confirmed.

Wouldn't he be happier if he went to Gateway or MENCAP?

We took him to them all – but it's so sad – he don't like them. Once we went to pick him up and he was sat all on his own in a corner and I said to the man that was in charge of it – 'this isn't what we bought him down for' – he said 'he will not join in'.

Trevor, Did you like the ATC when you went to see it? No. *Why not, you went to school with those people didn't you?* Yes. *But you didn't like them?* No. *Why not, did you think you could do more than the people you went to school with?* **Yes.** *Did you like school?* **Yes –**

MUM: They had Down's Syndrome there? *Do you know what Down's Syndrome is Trevor?* **Er...**

You do know them don't you – we've got one who lives round here haven't we? Andrew he's Down's Syndrome – and a little girl round the back – called a mongol but not now, they're called Down's Syndrome. You don't know what that is?

TREVOR: **No.**

He used to have a little girl friend at school but he won't have her down now. He had her down to tea a couple of times at school – now he's home she's rung up a couple of times but he won't see her. I said Trevor – let's have her down to tea it would be company for you. He said no – he will not have her here.

Wouldn't you like to have her here – you could watch TV and wouldn't have to talk too much? **No.**

Ada

Ada, aged 28, worked two days a week in a large hotel and refused to associate with her peers with whom she had spent two years at college and also knew from Wentwood. Although her parents acquiesced, it put a strain on the family and left her mother worrying about Ada spending long days at home on her own while they are all out at work. Ada was at home on her own for the interview. Her mother was seen next day.

You used to go to the centre? Yes. *Why did you stop going* I didn't like it very much. *Why didn't you like it?* There wasn't much to do up there.

Is there any more to do here at home? Yes cleaning, cooking... *Do you like cleaning?* Yes. *Do you do any cooking?* Yes. *Did you have any friends at the centre?* Yes – *and what were they like?* They were all right.

When you stopped going to the centre was it because you were unhappy? Yes. *Did you tell the people at the centre that you were unhappy?* Yes I told them – *and what did they say?* Not a lot.

Did you tell your mum? Yes – *and what did she say?* Stay home here. *Mum doesn't mind you don't go?* No.

Do you like it better here? Yes. *Don't you get lonely by yourself?* Yes sometimes. *What do you do when you're lonely?* Not a lot – *would you like to do more?* Yes.

Did you go to the hotel when you were at the centre? Yes. *When you stopped did you still keep the job on?* Yes. *Have you got any friends at work?* I talk to someone – *but they're not friends –* no. *Have you got any friends at home.* No.

Mother

I think she's a very assured young lady in the house

I'm not very keen on that – it's only recently that she's been home on her own – my other daughter was made redundant last year and she hasn't found a job – it sounds terrible really but its been quite handy for me. Its only recently that she's been home on her own –

So she's on her own not because you want it but because that's the way it's happened –

It is a problem for me – she does go out with that Ann on a Thursday to an art class for a couple of hours. I don't know who Ann is, whether it's a proper job or voluntary I don't know. She takes her to the theatre and things every so often. Its a long day for her to be on her own. When she's on her own she sometimes goes to the neighbours or over to Tesco's shopping. When she goes out she knows not to talk to strange men but I think if someone was really nice to her – you don't know you know.

She's never done anything silly has she? She goes to work, Oxfam, shopping...

No, but you've still got that in the back of your mind. I think someone else with her other than me would let her do more – they say to me you should let her do it. I say it's all well and good but you're not sitting here worrying about it.

Brian

Brian, aged 28, lived on his own quite independently in a council flat and was totally reliant on Mabel, his key worker, who made daily visits to sort out his money and his food. Social services delivered meals on wheels two mornings a week. He worked without pay in a gardening job one morning a week. His keyworker had arranged for him to train with the local church football club one evening a week. He appeared to have no friends and no social life other than visits to his family and to the home of the key-worker who lived nearby. He was very lonely.

The interviewer phoned him two weeks before and he arranged the interview on a day and time convenient to himself and offered coffee. The day before the visit the interviewer was told by the manager of a group home that social workers usually visited him in twos and that the flat was an indescribable mess. She also offered to phone up social services to see if it was safe to go unaccompanied. This did little for the interviewer's confidence (as the Wentwood records also indicated evidence of disruptive behaviour) who nevertheless decided to stay with the original arrangement, but go to a nearby pub to talk, and spend as little time as possible talking in the flat.

Brian turned out to be a tall good looking gangling 28-year- old with well styled curly hair, nicely dressed in jeans and a spotless white shirt. His manners were impeccable and although coffee was set out ready, he decided that the pub would be a better option and painstakingly cleared everything away before going out. The flat was immaculate. Amazingly courteous on the walk to the pub, he held doors and gates open, found a table, sitting the interviewer down before he too sat down. On arrival at the pub it transpired he been been banned at some earlier stage for disruptive behaviour!

Did you like Wentwood? No, I didn't like it much, I didn't get on with people. *Why not?* I got this temper with them – *You got bad tempered with them?* Yes – I was unhappy there.

You're not unhappy living on your own? No 'cause I'm independent. Got everything I want here – my music. *It's a lovely flat – do you ever have anybody in, visitors* – no, only Mabel [key worker].

Did you not feel you were independent in Wentwood? No *Why didn't you ask if you could leave Wentwood?* I did. *What happened?* In the end I left – *but you stayed two years* – I did not get on with the staff.

Did you live at home with your family before you went? No. *Where?* School. *You went away to school?* Yes. *Were you happy when you left Wentwood?* No. *Are you happy now?* I'm happy now, six months I've been here. *Before you came here where were you?* A children's home – thing was I used to live in a children's home.

How often do you see your family? The second week – *every second week* – no every month, second week.

Go back to friends – I've got Jack at work – he's got his own flat like me – he's independent like me.

Where did he go before? To a day centre. Jack was an old mate of mine, school-days.

You don't go to a day centre? No. *Why not?* I don't get on with the people there? *You seem to get on very well with me, why don't you get on with them?* It goes back to school days – *you mean the centre is like it was at Wentwood?* Yes – *and what didn't you like about that?*

The people – and the staff shout too much – I don't like that.

David

David, aged 22, appeared to have totally defeated his family and after some years they reached an equilibrium which enabled him to spend most of the day in bed, getting up at about two o'clock in the afternoon and spending the next two hours in the bathroom getting washed and dressed. He was diagnosed as brain damaged as a child and was in control of his own medication for epilepsy. He stayed alone in the house and didn't get up till his mother came back from work after lunch. He went to bed about three o'clock in the morning or whenever television finished. There appeared to be little in his life to motivate him to leave his bed and he had lost most of the skills he acquired at Wentwood from lack of practice. On leaving Wentwood, with one of the highest scoring final assessments, he had a work experience placement at the local Co-op where he was very well thought of. Similar placements at Wentwood included a supermarket and a riding school; he received good progress reports from both.

The main problem for his family would appear to be that he refused to have any contact with other learning disabled people or take any part in the multiplicity of such opportunities provided in his own city. He remained firmly in bed throughout the interview and refused to get up as it was too early, at mid day. However he answered questions sensibly, confirming most of the facts about his life already described by his parents.

Why do you stay in bed so long in the morning – why don't you get up? I like to have a lie in. *What time do you lie in until?* Lunch time. *Does Mum phone you when she's at work?* Yes she phones me from the office – *and what does she say are you going to get up today – and what do you do* – go back to sleep! *Why, she didn't say time to go back to sleep did she?* No. *What did she say?* Time to get up – *and why didn't you get up?* I'm not quite sure.

PARENTS: To be quite honest we've tried everything – at the Co-op the staff there still ask after him – would he like to come back – I said I don't want any money for him. He had a super time there – I'm sure he could get up to get there in the afternoon but in reality it's a working household with other people to consider and we've got to the state now that if there's no hassle – it's worth a lot.

He doesn't want to work and how do you make him? When he does something he does it well and if he wants to do it he will do it thoroughly. The MENCAP Pathway officer came and asked him he wanted to work and he said no. He won't go to Gateway and he won't relate to mentally handicapped people at all. It would be a lot easier if he would. He doesn't want anything to do with them – he'll pick up the slightest abnormality. He was unhappy at Wentwood. He wouldn't mix with the type of people that were there and I said once we got him home we'd never send him away again. He enjoys his own company. I think he did enjoy the Co-op when he was there – the little snippets that came back – there were a few incidents. Some of the younger girls were a bit unkind to him and would lose patience with him and perhaps, where we'd take it as a joke, they would go on and on. He found that very, very, difficult to cope with. On the other hand some of the more mature people were extremely kind to him and he relates very much to that.

He belongs to a church. As soon as he came home from Wentwood – to keep his training going – I went to see the vicar. They have a 14–18-year-old youth club where he goes. That's the main thing in his life. He goes twice week on Friday evening and Sunday evening. Sometimes he goes to church – it depends who is going from the club – but if he doesn't they meet afterwards at eight o'clock. He is the only handicapped person there – they're very good with him. He walks back between ten and half past or we go and get him.

It's sad, he's got the body of a man and he obviously fancies girls – and the times he phones them up and says will you come round to my house to play sort of thing – well you can understand them – he's very much wanting contact with them and it's hard for him, the frustration. He's going to take it out on his nearest and dearest, which is us. If we introduced him to one of the girls from Wentwood he would just not want to know. It wouldn't be a case of introducing them gradually – it would be a complete shut off.

Julie

Julie, as shown in Chapter 4, was a tall good looking, fashionable 24-year-old who has worked in an electrical firm for five years. Although she had always been within the special education system her school reports indicated that she found it difficult to talk to her peer group. The same complaint arose when she visited MENCAP and other clubs for learning disabled people. Although not academically able, she demonstrated good powers of concentration and was a sensible conversationalist. She appeared to find it frustrating to mix with other learning disabled people even at Wentwood, although less able than many of them. She had since lost many skills. However, she had a good social life with her family and their friends in the small village where they live.

Did you like Wentwood? No *Why not?* No good there. *Why not?* Didn't like things we did. *What did you do that you didn't like?* Don't know. *You liked going to the sports centre?* Yes. *Did you ride your bike?* Yes – *and did you ride a horse?* Yes.

What was wrong with that – you like those things – would you rather live at home? Yes. *You didn't like living there?* No, had to do dinner. *Do you like it better at home?* Yes.

What did you do at home that you didn't do at Wentwood? Go to work. *I think you went to work there too – yes. What did you do?* I went to a lady. *Did you help her clean?* No I laid the tables – went on a bus.

Do you go on a bus now? No – its difficult *Would you like to go back to Wentwood?* NO. *Did you have any friends at Wentwood?* No, not really friends.

(MUM: She used to go to the Olympic club.)

I've stopped that. *Don't you like it?* You don't meet anybody else there – I don't like them. *You don't like the people?* No. *Why didn't you like them – were they a bit silly* – Yes, very silly. *What did you do there?* Dancing, cards, wrestle. *Did you tell Mum you didn't like it or just stop or what?* I didn't like it.

MUM: She kept saying they didn't have any new records, one lad down there had a foul mouth and she didn't like that and there was a lot of them smoked down there that she didn't like.

Nick

Nick, aged 25, was the only ex-student who mixed easily with both able and disabled people. He lived at home in the main street of a small town and was part of large happy family of ten brothers and sisters. The mother was from a larger family and met her army husband when he was serving overseas. As can be seen, Nick recognised the hostility of the outside world whilst still wishing to join in. Good communication skills mask his disability and even with an IQ of 41 he has the insight to be aware that security is to be found at home with his family where he is accepted – rather than in the world of his less disabled peers.

The interview took place in the one large living room which resembled a gipsy caravan with an attractive profusion of knick knacks and china housed behind glass display cases on top of which were similar displays of assorted sporting trophies acquired by his siblings. Twenty-five grandchildren swelled the family from time to time and the forthcoming Christmas festivities were to be celebrated in shifts over three days. His mother had recently been on a three month 'round the world trip' to visit her own large extended family and some of her married daughters. Nick had been looked after by his father and brothers during this time. Nick was a small dark strange looking young man who had lost many skills through lack of practice since leaving Wentwood.

Towards the end of his two years at Wentwood they had managed to cure his nightly bed wetting but he had he had relapsed after three months back home and still wet his bed nightly. His family appeared unperturbed about this and felt that it may well be an intractable function of his medical condition. The interview took place amid much laughter as the family joined in – but still were careful to give Nick time and space to say what he felt.

Did Wentwood make him independent?

MUM: It's living in a big family really – they do learn a lot more. (BROTHER: we taught him all his alphabet and to count before he actually started school.) He didn't do very well at school – he was too busy looking at everyone else and what they were doing– he never got anything learnt himself. He's good at reading, but whether he understood what he read was another story. Wentwood was to teach him to look after himself –

And did it? Within reason. He learned to cook a bit – *but he doesn't do it* – no – it's always Mam can I go out – can I go for a ride – can I go to town?

You reckon it's the family that have brought him to the stage he is?

MUM: Definitely. At the hospital they told me at birth that he was brain damaged and would never learn. But having the next one was good, he was able to copy her – he was never able to walk or anything till she did. He couldn't even sit up but he copied the other one – following her, whatever she did, he did more or less. The only thing is he lacks concentration. He can do things but not for very long. You have to tell him to do everything every day.

Do you ever go to a disco? Yes I do, I'm going to one this Friday. *Where?* In town. (MUM: He usually goes to Gateway but he goes occasionally to D— [a stately home in the locality]. *What happens there?* It's a night club? *Who do you go with?* On my own.

MUM: We take him and bring him back.

This is the ordinary disco, anybody can go? Yes. *He goes to Gateway disco and also to the ordinary one?* Yes.

When you go to D— what do you do? Just sit down and have a chat. *Have you got any girl friends?* No, not at the moment. *Do you have girl friends?* Yes.

MUM: Every now and then he has a girl friend.

Do you like the disco at D—? Yes. *How much does it cost to go in?* Nothing I don't have to pay at all. *Doesn't it cost anything to go in?*

MUM: Yes but they let him in because they know him – he knows the bouncers and they let him in. He had a job there to do washing up but he talked to everybody else instead of working – he lasted for a week – it didn't work out.

Do you ever go to church?

Oh yes, every Sunday. I've been a server all my life. I normally get up at 8 o'clock on Sundays, mass is at 10.30.

MUM: He rides his mountain bike into town – he goes on the the train to work. *By himself?* Yes.

What else do you do? Biking. *Who with?* My friends. *Where do you meet them?* I normally meet them in the park.

Are they disabled in any way?

MUM: No. Mark is very good. everybody knows him, everybody. He
      doesn't know who they are, no names or anything but they're friends,
      he knows everybody. He goes to an ordinary youth club as well as
      Gateway...

Do you like Gateway club? Yes it's really good there – MENCAP and Gateway.
What do you do about holidays? I go with the Gateway club once a year.

Where do you go? Different places, Cumbria – the year before that I went
over to the Isle of Wight. *Do you find the friends you meet in Gateway talk as
easily as you?* Yes they do, they all does talk with me. *Are some of them rather
handicapped – a bit disabled?* No, not really.

Do you go to pubs – yes the one over the road, every night. *You go on your
own, what do you drink when you get there?* Coke, that's all I drink there.

MUM: He can answer the phone very well (BROTHER:he even gives you a
      message somebody phoned for you!) Yes he's very articulate!

*He spoke to me on the phone and did very well. They're not very nice to you here
at home – I wonder why you want to stay!*

      I love it here. I want to stay with my Mum. She don't want to let no-none
      hurt me or anything.

I'm sure she doesn't – she doesn't.

Is that why you like being here?

      I feel safe when I'm with my Mum. When I'm not – you know – things
      do get out of hand.

In what way? When I go out to D— the DJ always calls me monkey.

When you go to the disco? When I go to the actual disco. *And what do you say
when he calls you monkey?* I say I'm not so just leave it – *and what does he say
to that.* He calls me bubbles.

Nick's clothes all came from charity shops and his bedding had to be washed
daily. Records from the two years at Wentwood indicate they were unable to
lengthen his concentration span and that he was unable to complete any task
without constant reminders. Yet he was popular with both staff and students
and, surprisingly, considered relatively able. Nick was the last student to be
interviewed in the sample and the only one who was totally happy in his
environment and able to mix confidently with all his peers.

DISCUSSION

There has as yet been little recognition, in the relevant literature, of the alienation experienced by some learning disabled people when they finish their education and start their adult life within the community. This alienation was recognised by both parents and staff associated with that group of people in the research sample, who would have absolutely no contact with their obviously mentally handicapped peers. This group had all been to special schools and there was no ambiguity as to their original educational diagnosis. These people were aware that they had been to such schools and had enjoyed their school days but regarded them as something 'other' that now had no bearing on their adult life.

There was no indication, in this particular sample, that the people living in group homes clearly catering for people with developmental disabilities had a similar problem. Staff did report rare examples amongst other residents. The group home residents who were interviewed comprised 37 per cent of the total sample and seemed to have active and enjoyable social lives bound up with Gateway clubs and the various holiday and social opportunities provided by MENCAP and the different religious groups such as Faith and Light. It was those people living at home, or independently, who would appear to lead alienated lives on the fringes of a community from which they are unwillingly set apart.

The young adults in this project are amongst the first generation to experience the benefits of the 1971 Education Act with its emphasis on pre-school and full time education for children with developmental disabilities. They were taught by teachers who were, for the first time, correctly trained in the particular skills appropriate for the education of people with learning disabilities. Many of the sample have also spent a short time in mainstream education. They are also amongst the first people to take advantage of specially designed courses in Colleges of Further Education and this particular group of people are unique in that they have experienced the two year residential sixth form non-vocational social education curriculum offered by Wentwood before going on to such colleges.

At Wentwood the majority of students benefited from a variety of work experience placements in the local community which they still remember with pleasure many years later. Their recall of aspects of the work were accurate when compared with the records, and they even remembered the buses they travelled on and the route to work. As shown in other chapters, after leaving Wentwood over half the sample have again been involved in either full or part-time employment alongside their non-disabled peers. Yet the majority of these people still enjoy the contact they have with their similarly disabled friends in their the various clubs and group homes.

Because the sample had all completed the same two year training course and there are such complete records and assessments for this group, it is possible to say with confidence that there is little indication that these feelings of isolation are a function of either higher ability or a particular syndrome or home background. Many people with proved higher intellect were well settled in group homes and, working or not, had formed strong and close friendships with other residents. Several Wentwood students had gone on together to group homes and some of these friendships dated back to early school days. This was not surprising as the geographical catchment area of Wentwood was mainly limited to the adjoining counties of Wiltshire, Avon, Buckinghamshire and Hertfordshire.

SALIENT ISSUES

There seems to be no rational explanation for the unexpected finding of alienation in 20 per cent of the sample. Those closest to the people concerned could offer no reason as to why their children, who had been happily educated within the special education system should develop, as young adults, a sudden dislike of their similarly disabled peer group. Further research is needed into this group of people as this project could find no common factor within the group.

CHAPTER 5

Case Studies

LIZZIE

It would be encouraging to present case studies of the many able Wentwood ex-students who having made good progress during their Wentwood course, continued to do so after Wentwood and currently live relatively independent lives within a community setting. This history is that of Lizzie the ex-student with the lowest base line score on entry to Wentwood and the lowest final leaving score of the entire sample. She was only ever able to be assessed on the lowest assessment form, which could be completed by a child of average intelligence during their first year in infant school. Of the 120 social skills needed to complete this assessment, on arrival at Wentwood, Lizzie had a baseline score of only 44 skills. The final assessment, two years later, indicated an increase of only 4 skills, giving a total score of 48.

Wentwood records show that Lizzie never reached the stage of being able to be taught with the other students, nor did they feel that her developmental level indicated that she was ready for such teaching. Wentwood designed three individual behaviour modification programmes in an attempt to overcome her main problems. These were defined in the Wentwood records as hitting people, disruptive behaviour, tantrums to extricate herself from jobs she chose not to do, falling asleep when not stimulated, and what was loosely termed 'non-social attitudes'.

Wentwood persevered for one year with these programmes noting that when she was frustrated she would either be aggressive or rip her clothes. They constantly looked for new ways to increase her motivation to stop her falling asleep. Throughout the records there were clear indications that on her own terms Lizzie was capable of surprisingly effective behaviour. One despairing comment after a term of little recordable progress was that *'on her own terms, and when she is in the mood, there's no student with a more natural ability to anticipate what needs doing when'*.

Throughout the time at Wentwood Lizzie was deemed to have dormouse behaviour except when being stimulated on a one-to-one basis. It is clear from the records that although there was little observable recorded progress the implementation of such an intense socialisation program provided Lizzie with an excellent foundation for adult communal living.

In current terminology Lizzie would be described as having *challenging behaviour* but this term could well be accepted as modest English under-statement for the variety of challenges she presented in a communal living environment. At the time of the follow up, some eight years later when living in a Home Farm Trust establishment, Lizzie had increased her self-help score by one level bringing it up to level three. By this time the majority of the ex-students were functioning at levels eight and nine.

On arrival at the Home Farm Trust Lizzie was virtually mute, aggressive and obsessed with eggs. For years she had been stealing eggs, sticking her finger in and drinking the egg whilst keeping the shells intact. She often kept eggs in her room. A new member of staff, who had been a farmer, watched her carefully and in a moment of inspiration introduced her to the local egg farm who were amazed at her skill. She is now one of their more skilled workers and sorts, grades and rejects hundreds of eggs daily. As the Home Farm Trust is a charity it was decided she would be paid in eggs rather than money. This proved difficult as, according to staff, she ate her wages. How-ever, she was eventually persuaded to return the eggs to the kitchen having first taken them to her room on arriving home from work.

Her work now provides eggs for her house and also provides her with pocket money. As well as working, Lizzie enjoys riding and animal therapy sessions. These are designed to give disabled people confidence and do constructive work with animals in a realistic environment. Without the for-tuitous meeting with the member of staff concerned, she would certainly not have found such appropriate work with eggs and may well still have been spending time in her room sucking eggs as a pleasurable occupation. One of the main points of interest in this case study is that there was no psychological intervention at any time in Lizzie's life.

Lizzie still has few communication skills, is incapable of sustained conver-sation and goes to sleep when bored. The interview was not only a challenge but the interviewer was somewhat disconcerted when Lizzie displayed a certain amount of aggression, relieving her feelings on her television set, the mattress of her bed, and finally going to sleep.

The case study is presented purely by the protagonists because all too often we forget the wider impact that people with challenging behaviour have on their families, friends, local communities, churches, schools, holiday makers, leisure provisions and (in the unlikely event of their obtaining work) work-places. Convention subsumes them at various stages in their life within the medical model, educational model, care in the community model or whatever provision they are currently accepting. Lizzie's case history should make us question our assumptions about the quality of life for such people. Out of the entire sample of ex-students, Lizzie would appear to have found the quality of life most suited to her needs.

Throughout this book the students' names have been changed to preserve their anonymity. Lizzie's parents were happy for her real name to be used. Lizzie was 26 at the time of the interview.

Lizzie
Parents' Life History of Lizzie

'Lizzie was born on the 9th August 1967 all very swiftly but uneventfully – it wasn't what you call a precipitate labour but after birth she went blue. She was nursed in an incubator for that night and the following morning. She was seen by a paediatrician and brought to me the next morning as he said that all was well. She was a very good baby which was just as well as I had a very energetic toddler of 16 months at the time. We moved house when she was just six weeks old so she really was ideal for the job as she didn't make great demands.

We started wondering if there might be something slightly amiss when she was about six months. We always used to take the children out with us for supper when we were going to friends and before we went home we would usually get them up and have a little play and compare notes with our various friends. On this particular occasion our friends had got a boy of the same age as Liz. He was got up and Liz was got up and they were sitting on their respective mothers' knees and I noticed that Fergus was playing with his mother's necklace and looking at the lights and Liz was just sitting there and she seemed to be not taking particularly much interest.

Then a little bit later on we heard of another friend whose child of the same sort of age was missing milestones and was found to have a heart condition so we thought we'd better investigate it. This we did, and the paediatrician said he thought she had a storage disease as she had an enlarged spleen. He said it might not be, and recommended that we wait until she was about a year old. My husband's parents, his father was a doctor, were very anxious that we should get this cleared up. I don't think they felt there was anything wrong or even knew very much about storage disease – nobody seemed to – but they thought that it would be better to know. When Liz was ten months old she went up to Great Ormond Street Hospital and she stayed there for a month. During that time I think everybody who went through the door of the hospital also went past Liz because she was something of a mystery who didn't fit into any category. At the end of this period when we ultimately went and saw the specialist he said that it wasn't a storage disease. She had general brain damage but they couldn't give us any reason. They couldn't give us any indication how she would develop – what was going to happen – but we were just so relieved she wasn't going to die – sort of fairly swiftly – that at that time we hadn't considered too much further forward. The only thing that got particularly interesting, and everybody was very curious about, was that apparently she's got some special palm lines and this was looked at by all sorts of specialists with genetic interests. Again there wasn't any conclusion reached on that.

Feeding wise we had a big problem teaching her to drink from a cup as I was a bit lazy. Having fed the children myself we went straight from me onto a feeding cup at around six months. During the time of the changeover Liz was meant to be helping herself and learning to drink from the cup and holding it herself. She resisted and I know we had about three days when I was sort of biting my nails and thinking 'come on – she's got to do this' and finally my mother persuaded her to pick it up and take it, but she wasn't ever particularly wanting to pick things up – she was a bit lazy. The same thing happened with learning to sit – she could sit being balanced in a sitting position and stay there, but she didn't make great efforts to sit up herself.

Walking became a problem – she learned to roll and I would make her roll from one end of the garden to another – mud and rain notwithstanding. We made suitable clothing so she could do that because otherwise she would get absolutely no exercise at all. She became very proficient at rolling around, so once she'd achieved one thing she really didn't seem to see any great reason for progressing to the next. Walking was only really achieved by physical effort on our part. From frog-marching her round the village – mostly in the early hours of the morning when we could do it quietly without any body noticing – as we thought – because I'm sure that if the NSPPCC would have been around they would have said we were being cruel and we would have been in big trouble. (Some people complained about an escaped cow wandering round the village in the early morning but we said it was Lizzie!) Learn to walk she did, and now she is a very good walker and there's no problem. For years when we were on holiday if we were going for a walk she always yelled vigourously for about the first three quarters of an hour and you just had to pretend that was some sort of modern music or something and get on with it because there was no other way. You had to hold her hand to keep her going or otherwise she would have just stopped.

She went to school at three years and one month. We're not quite sure how this happened because we hadn't really called on social workers or asked for any help from other agencies because we seemed to be coping all right and we had a very supportive doctor. There wasn't a problem – if we needed help we got it. We would take her to school and then go and fetch her. When we went for our official interview the headmaster had a report about this child who was very backward and wasn't talking or doing anything for herself. She wasn't walking, wasn't potty trained and he thought this was just going to be a cabbage going straight into special care. Having been carried into his study when we sat down Liz climbed off my lap – she was crawling by that stage. She crawled round and climbed up onto his knee, climbed up onto the desk and started playing with his pipe. He was rather amused and said there was no way she could possibly go into special care and was going to be the one exception to the rule. They didn't have children who were not potty trained going into classes. She went straight into the nursery class rather than special care.

From there she progressed with the school. Hyperactive at a walk and only doing things that she saw purpose in doing. She would stack up cups and saucers after they had their break and take those back to the kitchen but she wouldn't pile up bricks. She saw no point. She was tested in all sort of ways. She was in hospital and she was involved with various people but they never came up with anything particular when she was assessed. As a very little girl they were always intrigued how in the morning when she woke up her bed was always full of biscuit crumbs. It transpired that she would creep past the office (where they sat watching through the night to make sure that everybody remained in their wards) go into the kitchen, get a stool, climb onto the stool, onto the work surface, get the biscuit tin, help herself and return to bed the same way. They never saw her do it.

She was always observant in things about the home and she had no sense of danger. We got some quite exciting happenings when for example somebody was doing something on the roof and left the ladder unattended. The next thing I knew she was at the top of the ladder. Well of course you had to get terribly, terribly, cross because if she realised she was at risk she might have become frightened. So I used to get absolutely furious and shout at her to come down – what was she doing very naughty and all this – until she came down. She climbed out of her bedroom window on top of the greenhouse roof one time and walked along that. How she didn't break the glass we'll never know and as a result all our upstairs rooms got bars and wire netting to keep Elizabeth in. Our house was slightly like Fort Knox but for keeping people in rather than keeping people out. She was a climber and interested in that sort of activity without wanting to learn to do things particularly – excepting food wise.

She learned how to boil a kettle and I think a lot of people thought we were very foolish letting her risk this but we felt that anything she was actually interested in we had to promote, because if we'd stopped it she would just have sat back and said – 'oh I won't bother'. She learned how to make a cup of tea or coffee. She learned where things lived: plates, dishes and that sort of thing. She learned which was the flour – which was the sugar and always when I was cooking she would help – she would get things – not always the right thing but usually the right thing. In that respect it was good.

They had some problems at school and I also had problems with her becoming aggressive. If she were told off she would come and hit me. If the teacher at school told somebody off she would would go and administer a slap to that person. One had to be very careful because she was very strong. The aggression made life a bit difficult, particularly as she got older. I had to always be on the look out because I'd get these swipes. One thing that I couldn't do – I couldn't ever put the car away in the garage because if I did she took umbrage and would come and thump the car or throw gravel at it. That made life a little bit traumatic. Other people could put the car away and there was no problem.

Inside the family she was just accepted as Elizabeth, you didn't think of her in terms of age or ability, she was just herself. At this time we had four children and we had no problems with Liz being accepted by the boys or her not accepting them. She was just very much her own person within the unit of the family. From the time that the youngest brother started physically overtaking her we decided that we must have times away with the boys to give them freedom to do some things that she wouldn't enjoy. Before that time we used to do everything as a family unit whether it was swimming, or going in boats, or riding or walking or whatever. So she did experience a tremendous number of activities. When we were on holiday in Scotland I would take her riding. We got a special saddle with a bar at the front which stopped her from falling forwards if she did feel like it but also gave her something to hold on to. It had a high back as well but not like the special saddles that have been developed since then. I used to take the saddle up and we would put this on one of the ponies who was particularly friendly and she would ride. She never wanted to go exploring, walking with us, but she would do her own thing. One of the first times we found that she really was quite a good walker was when we lost her. We were on holiday and had a caravan on a farm and she would head off if she felt like it and escape. We heard this person shouting from the top of the lane – and Elizabeth had walked a couple of hundred yards up and crossed over the road and was happily playing with two very unfriendly farm collies. They were all rolling about the grass together. After that, where normally she would have got a lift down the lane, she was made to walk back up the lane because if she could do it because *she* chose to do it, then she could do it because *we* chose to do it. If she didn't she wouldn't get away with it.

She enjoyed everything the boys did and they enjoyed actually taking her. If they were canoeing they'd give her a ride in it. There was never any feeling that she should be left out and sometimes when we went away they would say 'surely Liz would enjoy this – she could do this' but we did gradually find that there were things that they enjoyed and she didn't, so they did come to accept that it was right that they should leave her behind. We tended to leave her during Easter time in respite care places. The hospital was very difficult because you had to go and get blood tests and stool tests and all the rest. She could have gone there but it was such a palaver that to go away for a weekend or a week, it was so much complication, that I preferred not to use them if it was possible. Also it was very much a hospital.

Before we got to that stage, when we could we exchanged children with our friends and Elizabeth was included in that. There people who were able to make their house or their doors secure so she couldn't get out. We would give her nights away so that when she actually went off to stay with people she wasn't unused to being away from home. It never bothered her at all. When they started the family support system where families would take a child – Liz was actually one of the first from her school to go away and stay with a family. We developed a very close friendship with them and they were wonderful and she enjoyed going to them. They enjoyed having her, I think, but we've lost touch with them now.

Things like potty training came very slowly but she was able to be trained and we gradually got rid of nappies finally going all night. In those days you were still using towelling nappies and we got to the stage where towelling nappies were getting too small. By the time she was just over five she was stopping wearing nappies at night. It didn't mean that we had dry beds at night. She had to be lifted about half past nine every night and that went on until she was well into her teens, because if you missed the time, then her bed would be wet. Now she is able to cope at nights and we don't have accidents at all.

She has always been very friendly and has a lot of friends around the village. We changed churches when she must have been about ten and started going to our local village church. Previously we had been going to a Presbyterian church and they had a creche and I used to leave Liz with the little ones. Then the little ones would be in church but Liz still went to the creche although she was much too old. When we started going in the village we gradually got her so that she would sit through the service. It's quite strange because the congregation used to get quite used to her making peculiar noises. She was never disruptive but sometimes she would make a yawn or a bit of loud exclamation of some sort. On occasions someone would say – 'I heard Elizabeth in church' and it hadn't been Elizabeth. She hadn't been in church at all but people became used to and expected it. She got to know all the people there and then she took on herself some jobs. She always had to go and put the candles out on the communion table and she always had to carry the cross back and put it in its place. She always had to open the door at the end and it was as much as anybody's life was worth to try and interfere with any of these jobs. This is still the same.

If she has a self-appointed task she does not want anybody to interfere and I think this is something that has come out with the egg picking. One of the helpers who took her on one of the days was trying to help her and she was very much pushing him away and indicating that this was her thing and he needn't interfere – it wasn't his job.

During all time until she went to Wentwood she was extremely healthy. She had the odd coughs and colds but nothing much. The exception to this being when she caught measles and she got a bit chesty after that. If she got a cold it tended to go onto her a chest so after that I kept the foot of her bed on blocks. Every time she went to bed she had her head tipped but it seemed to work and I think now – with the exception of the epilepsy that seems to be under control – she's as fit as could be.

There definitely were problems and it wasn't until she went away to Wentwood that I realised the pressure that I was living under. You needed to know where she was at all times because she would go out of the door and wander off. Bath University Engineering Department developed an electronic door lock for us because at one stage she learned how to manipulate keys. Although we kept the kitchen door locked she could turn the key. I kept the key on a string round my neck and then when the other boys were at home they would be outside and want to go to the loo or something. So I would have to come and open the door and then wait for them to go back and lock the door behind them. The electronic lock was coded and opened either from inside or outside and was absolutely brilliant. She also was an inhibiting factor in my sort of social life at school. When I went to collect the children it was much easier for me to stay in the car, because if I got out she would get out, and we didn't have straps and restraints like we have for children nowadays and it would have been difficult. So whereas other people would get out of the car and chat I tended to sit in the car because otherwise there would be a scene. If she were thwarted she would throw herself onto the ground and shout and scream and kick. She was quite big to physically man-handle.

Yet at the same time you did what you had to do and it's only in retrospect you think back and think 'well yes, how did I actually manage'. At the time it didn't seem quite such hard work. But at the same time, as she was older, you didn't actually find that people were saying 'Oh, it will be lovely, I'll have Elizabeth for a day and let you have some time off'. It was known that she needed constant watching and although they all accepted her for herself they didn't actually quite fancy dealing with her on her own without one of the family around to help.

We didn't initially think that the Home Farm Trust would be a possibility for Liz because she was below their minimum standard of requirement. We did put her name down at about two years old on their waiting list in the hopes that perhaps one day she would go. We went and had a look round with her when she was quite little and we liked the concept of living in the country in a community setting but not having the sort of town hustle and bustle. We're not really town people ourselves and she's very much prefers wellington boots and walking around in the fields, chasing cows, talking to the chickens or feeding the ducks or whatever. She actually has a very good relationship with all animals. In the New Forest she can always get up to ponies and talk to them whereas they would run away before we got to them. She was on scratching terms with the wild pigs in the forest. Strange animals are very good with her but we did slightly draw the line at the bull who used to live just over the fence when we were camping in Scotland. She would have been very happy to have gone and talked to it. It seemed the sort of setting we wanted for her.

Because we didn't think the Home Farm Trust was going to be possible, when it came nearer the time when we should be making decisions we took her to a Steiner community and then we had to go for interviews in London. They said she wasn't far enough advanced for one of their adult communities. We made many, many inquiries and we weren't actually coming up with anything very much. Then suddenly the Home Farm Trust said that they were going to broaden their horizons and that Elizabeth would be acceptable. We pinned all our hopes on them. Avon had taken Liz into a hostel after she left Wentwood, to see if Wentwood had pushed her forward far enough so that she could look after herself and then go to a day centre and live in a hostel. We didn't what her to move away from home exactly but we were feeling that we wanted to make sure she was settled. Hostel living wasn't what we were looking for. We had to go though the motions before Avon would see that what we were wanting was what we thought was the best thing for her.

Anyway, they did take her to a hostel for a fortnight's assessment and when she wasn't being stimulated she sat in a corner and vegetated. They were very short of staff at the day centre and she was put in the special care unit. She sat in a corner and sucked her thumb unless somebody was working with her and trying to make her do something. At the end of this time we had an assessment from Avon and they said they were very sorry but they didn't have anything in the county that they felt was suitable for Elizabeth. They knew we'd had the offer of a place with the Home Farm Trust and they did agree with us that the high staff student relationship was going to be to Elizabeth's benefit and advantage, so they were prepared to fund her. We were delighted.

There haven't been any great dramatics – it's all very mundane really – just the everyday story of the Gibson family if you like!

Home Farm Trust

Lizzie's interview was carried out almost entirely with the staff of the Home Farm Trust. Lizzie was present throughout the entire day but declined to answer until the very end. She appeared to be following the general conversation. When bored she fell asleep as was her wont. The main respondent among the staff was the member of staff who found Lizzie her job. Although not her key-worker he was the key-worker of her boyfriend and knows them both very well. He has subsequently become her key worker.

Initially all the questions were addressed to Lizzie who showed interest but declined to respond. Her communication skills appeared to be virtually nil. Towards the end of a very long day Lizzie started to whisper a few single words in answer to questions. They were accurate and sensible

Staff

Lizzie lives in a house with five other people attached to the main hall. We have six members of staff who live on site and they do 'on call' from their own homes and we have a 'sleeping in' staff in house 7. We have an 'awake' night staff who would phone through to the house of the resident staff on call.

Two mornings a week Lizzie goes to work, she has a job collecting eggs. *You don't break them?* No she's very good. *Where does she go?* a farm about 10 miles from here. *How does she get there* – by car – *somebody takes her?* Yes.

Who showed her how to do it?

She picked it up as she went along. She has a passion for eggs so its not a great problem really.

Do you collect all the eggs – do you have to move all the hens?

No they come down a chute. She's in where they stack the eggs. She collects them in the big egg trays and nobody helps her there.

How did she get the job?

Well I realised that Lizzie had a passion for eggs and it suddenly came to me that perhaps she'd like to do that. She was doing it one day a week and then they offered her more.

Can anyone talk to her or understand her? She makes herself understood, conversations are not her strong point.

I don't like talking about her and not to her – she wouldn't be able to answer what you're asking.

It must be unique to have thought about that as a job.

Not really. When you get to know Lizzie you realise she's fanatical about eggs. If Lizzie found eggs she would make a hole and suck them raw. She was a perfectionist, she never broke them. Her room was full of them stacked up against the walls – as many as she could get.

Does she still? No she doesn't do that now – this is what amazed us. She likes an egg a day now.

Do they pay her?

Er – yes. Well what they do – they gave her a choice of having eggs or money. So when she went down one day a week she had two and a half dozen eggs – and then we thought that perhaps she'd like to have money for the second job – but she wasn't impressed with having money. So she now has five dozen eggs a week which she sells to the other houses – so she has the money but she has her own eggs.

Does she take them round to the other houses?

Well we come and buy them. It's very difficult with Lizzie because she wouldn't want to actually part with them. I don't think she would understand that eggs would go off – she would have them all stacked up against her bedroom wall. When she goes into the packing station which is adjacent to the farm – she thinks that's heaven. All these thousands of eggs. She gets five pounds which is a bargain for what she does – but it wouldn't make any difference to her if they paid her five hundred pounds a week. We feel its more important that she goes – rather than gets paid. It's very difficult – one of our people worked three full days a week on Lord – estate for a full wage – but it had to be reduced because of the money and the pension.

The tray holds two and a half dozen and she packs about a hundred dozen a morning. She grades them on top. She has to grade them – she has to pick out the cracked ones and the small ones.

Are there many cracked one Lizzie? [nods] *What do you do with the cracked ones?* [grunts] *Do you put them on a spare tray?* [nods] *At Wentwood they remember her as having some language which she used quite well.*

Yes, she's got some language but not conversation. She can make herself understood – she can tell you what she wants. If you ask her a question she can answer – sometimes.

Lizzie – are you going shopping? **SHOPPING.** *What are you going to buy?* [grunts] *Tell me about the eggs? Just say yes or no. Do you have a lot of broken eggs?* **YES.** *Do you hold them up to the light to look for cracks?* [grunt] *Do you break any?* [grunt].

She is very very capable – she's doing it well. They wouldn't have asked her to do more days if she wasn't. She's amazingly good at it – she's only broken about four eggs the whole time she's been there.

And it was you who actually twigged there might be something she could be doing – how long has she been here? I've been here three years and she was here before.

It's amazing that someone who appeared to be without any potential is doing so well.

If you asked Lizzie to get something she could go and get it. If she's inspired she's very capable – if she's not inspired she just walks out. I believe there is a job for everybody – somewhere out there for every single one of them there's a job that will suit them. Hers is one of the simplest jobs I've found –

Yet she'd been here years before you came.

What do you do about holidays?

Once a year we have a meeting with everybody. What we do, we set out tables and brochures of most types of holidays and we let them look round. There are 32 of them – and then we get an idea of who wants to do what. We then compile a list of who wants to go were and then come back to them...

How does Lizzie manage –

Well those that can't decide or talk – we have to go and talk to them and say, would you like to join this group? Every year there's an amount set aside for holidays, about £250. If they wanted to go to Disneyland and could afford it – and some of them can – then they could go there. We've got a whole range of abilities here. Lizzie went on a farm.

Did she choose that herself or did you steer her toward it?

She chose it herself. Lizzie goes to eggs twice a week and to animal therapy a day a week as well, which she pays for, but the eggs she gets pays for it. She goes to riding for the disabled Thursday evenings – it's indoors.

So she's very busy?

Yes. If you don't keep her busy she opts out. Tuesday night she goes to Gateway club. She likes walking and shopping. She's been to the races a few times and usually goes to the county shows and point-to-points. A member of staff takes not more than two of them. Most days she's out somewhere – Monday she goes shopping. She goes to keep fit in the town. There's no bedtime, they can stay up till 12 or 1 o'clock but its not encouraged. They sleep in weekends until lunch time if they want, it doesn't matter about breakfast. If she likes a certain member of staff she'll get up early to be with her on a Sunday.

Has she got any friends outside the home – no – or does she ask anybody back here? No. Phil, the lad who's just walked through is Lizzie's best friend. *Her boyfriend?* Yes, he doesn't say a lot either. *Do you and Phil ever go out shopping together?* Yes sometimes. They went on their holidays together – the farming holiday. *Phil likes horses?*

Yes, that's why they are friends. She has no friends apart from the family. If you asked the majority of our residents where they would rather be – here or anywhere else – they always say home.

They don't call this their home?

No, very few. Those that can speak will say 'I am going home' and 'I am coming back'. The Home Farm Trust is very parent-orientated The governors are all parents. The people I am key worker to all say 'I am going home'– meaning home.

Do you encourage that? No. We encourage them to say this is home. *When do they make the break?* I don't know, I presume that when their parents are no longer alive. *Nobody has yet?* No.

Lizzie, if you're unhappy who do you tell? **I DON'T TELL** [first sentence in the whole day]

She's very impulsive aren't you Liz? We all know when she's unhappy because she throws things around and cart-wheels and things – and that's not a problem because we know when she's unhappy.

She was getting that way in the bedroom with us? Yes. *How do you deal with her?*

> We ignore it and then she soon comes round. We found that's the best way because she doesn't stay angry very long.

I can't really ask her the next question because she won't answer – Lizzie is there anything that you want to do that you can't do? **NO.** *That was clear enough!*

[Lizzie goes to sleep]

> This is what she does when she gets bored – she goes to sleep. Did she do that at Wentwood? She does need a lot of motivating. We did had a problem with her at the beginning – she spent most of the day asleep.

> Her boyfriend Phil – he has no comprehension of money at all. I'm his keyworker. If I take him out we have to work out what he wants and then I draw the money and go and buy that and get the receipt and take it back. Lizzie usually gives us her purse to lock in the car when we go shopping.

Do they all do that? No. Lizzie does, she prefers us to look after her purse.

Does she wash her own hair? She doesn't wash it but she does dry it herself with her own dryer. *Do you bath yourself –* I think the ladies have to help her because she's not all that keen on water. *Don't you have a shower after riding like you did at Wentwood?*

> If she's reminded she bathes but she doesn't do it for herself. She wouldn't change her clothes unless we tell her. She dresses herself but we sort of tidy her up.

What about washing or hand washing? Everything goes in the washing machine because we just haven't got time. *If it doesn't go in the washing machine it doesn't get bought?*

> That's about the size of it, yes. Lizzie can use the washing machine herself and she can get her own cornflakes and toast. She's one of the few who can.

At the end of the day, although many staff had helped with information, an interesting three-way discussion arose between the author, the co-ordinator of the unit, and John who, although not Lizzie's key-worker had found her the egg job. As both their views were similar, and they often finished each others sentences. their views have been merged. The majority of staff spoken to seemed to espouse a similar philosophy.

What proportion of people can you actually get out of here to somewhere outside, regardless of what they get paid? Very few.

The aim here isn't to get people out into the community is it? They stay here and this is their home.

Not any more. It used to be. The Home Farm Trust was organised to provide a home for life. In current political terms we can't do that now, because the funding isn't always there and we haven't got the money to guarantee that.

Surely local authority funding will continue as long as they are here won't it?, even if they don't send you more people?

Not necessarily. Several have now said that they have provisions nearer, in their own county – and cheaper... Nobody has actually pushed us to the limit yet – but that's what they are going to do.

Have you got anybody here who is self-funding? Yes. *And what does that cost a year?* £22,000 a year – £420 a week. *How can anybody be self-funding?* Trust funds.

For their own self esteem we try to get them out somewhere. We can try to get them into the community on a daily basis – if not to live out there. There are a couple of them that we think may not be here for the rest of their lives. I think it's the living on their own that's the problem. I can't envisage even our most able living without any support in the community. Those that do are not living in the community really. They're living on their own. Looking at ours – they'd maybe sit down for a meal because one of them would be more able and cook it – but come the end of the meal and it's cleared up – they'd all go off to their bedroom and there would be no-one there to generate some conversation or a game or go to the pub or whatever – they wouldn't and couldn't.

I don't think anyone thought through the Care in the Community policy. They went for it because it was going to be cheaper. It's all right in theory – it's the practicality that was wrong

How do you see this as being different to anywhere else? What's your staff ratio?

One to six. Probably over all it's not. In a shift you probably have one member of staff to the residents in each house but the total staff we probably have is 50 staff to the same number of residents because we've got instructors and night staff. Every week we have parents of three- and four-year-old children coming to look round and wanting to put them down for later.

All we see ourselves as doing is developing people as far as they are capable of. We see our job as enabling them to reach their true potential whatever that is. There isn't much else you can do – is there?

GILLIAN

Gillian, aged 26, is a small obese lady with Down's Syndrome and a congenital hip dislocation that makes walking very difficult, although she manages to walk everywhere. For the last five years she has lived in a small semi-detatched house in a new town, with two other ladies who appear to be rather more able. However, Gillian lives almost totally independently with key worker support. A key-worker comes in one day a week to help her do her washing and to bath her and she relies on her mother to cut her fingernails...
Although she can manage a shower herself she has difficulty getting out of the bath unaided. She is also not allowed to use the washing machine on her own.

Gillian remains in close contact with her parents who have separated but still live in the vicinity, and sees them both weekly. Father is active on the local council and her mother is in one of the caring professions. Gillian has always been within the special education system and attended the local training Centre as well as Wentwood where she was one of the more able students. She came straight to the small group home after leaving Wentwood, where she has been for five years. She dislikes the group home intensely.

Although Gillian claims to hate her life in the home, there was lots of laughter when she was initially interviewed with the two other residents present. As can be seen the story changed after their departure. Both the other ladies have jobs and Gillian also works at a local charitable foundation two days a week and has a full timetable attending art group, Bible classes and various other occupations. She reads, writes and can write down familiar phone numbers, travels on her own by bus both locally and into town but chooses to go to her doctor with a social worker.

The three ladies do all their own shopping and go together to the local supermarket once a week to buy their food. The supermarket has only convenience foods and potatoes and they do not have fresh meat. After the weekly shopping has been budgeted for and completed the they each keep their own money. The local fish and chip shop is used when they prefer not to cook or are late back home. Unusually Gillian talks to the neighbours and plays with their children. The house is well organised with separate calenders for each lady on a notice board on the kitchen which also lists all the relevant phone numbers they may need. There is a weekly cooking rota displayed; further inspection revealed that little cooking was actually attempted: they mainly reheated convenience foods. Holiday arrangements were also on a list and the three appeared to be going to Butlins with a social worker. This was their annual group holiday which they all enjoyed. Gillian also had other holidays with her parents, camping with her father and going to stay with her siblings with her mother, but these paled into insignificance when she was describing the fairground and discos at Butlins!

The case history is presented in the order in which it was obtained. The author initially was very impressed with Gillian's lifestyle. The house seemed ideally located in relation to shops, transport and the small scale of her part of the new town estate with gardens for each house and pedestrian walkways. Gillian's independence when the author joined her to go shopping was quite remarkable – as was her good humour and easy manner with the supermarket staff. Unusually, Gillian was well able to understand the financial implications of her life and her lifestyle seemed appropriate and virtually independent. She appeared to be living the 'ordinary life' as envisaged in the original blue print of that name.

Closer inspection revealed a very different truth and the author has chosen to do very little editing and present the everyday minutiae of Gillian's life as seen by the three protagonists – Gillian, her keyworker and her mother. Gillian's interview was carried out over several hours and the relevant areas are presented. Personal family details have been omitted. When the three perspectives are merged Gillian's life with the day-to-day decisions and their implications becomes very much a construct of the confabulations of significant others – a fact which her mother would now appear to be regretting.

Gillian's Interview

What do you like doing best? Knitting. *Do you like house work?* I clean my own room – take turns in cleaning the rest.

If things go wrong and you're unhappy who do you tell? Alice [keyworker] *You don't tell your Mum?* No. *Why not* – I don't want to tell my Mum.

What do you do at work? Garden shop – *what do you do there* – I clean up – *do you like that* – yes – *Do you go to Gateway club or any sort of club?* N— Club On Thursday – it starts at 7 o'clock... *Do you all go?* Only me – *how do you get there* – I get a taxi. *Do you pay the taxi* – yes. *How much is it?* £2 *How do you get back?* By coach. *What do you do there?* Games.

How do you go into town? Catch two buses – change – to city centre. *By yourself?* Yes – it's easy. *When do you go?* Any time. *What time do you get up in the morning?* Quite early about 7 o'clock. *Do you ever stay in bed at the weekends* – sometimes. *What time do you go to bed?* Any time – about eleven I think.

How do you work out your money? I go to the post office – *and take all your money out?* Yes – *in pound notes* – yes – *how much is it?* £74 – *Do you bring that home?* Yes. *What day do you go to the post office?* Tuesdays. *What do you do with the money?* Alice sorts it out.

You were good at money at Wentwood – yes – *so you do understand about change?* Yes. *Are you all good at money?* Yes. *Who taught you?* Wentwood. *Can you fill in forms?* Yes.

Who buys the food? We do. *All by yourself?* Yes *Where do you go?* Across the road – Tuesdays – all together in the morning. *Do you make a list?* We know what we want. *What sort of things do you buy?* All our own food – the three of us, we know what we're doing.

What do you get? Things for dinner. *Do you get the whole week's shopping?* Yes. *Where do you get the money from for it?* Alice sorts the money out on Tuesday. *Do you get your own money from the post office* – yes. *Do you find money very difficult?* Yes. *Do you know about change and things?* Yea, I'm all right.

Have you got your own bank book? Yep – *and you put the money in and take it out?* Yep. *You buy all the food between the three of you?* Yes – *can you all cook?* Yes. *Who does the cooking?* Sometimes I do it. *What do you cook?* Steak pie.

Who's cooking tonight? I am – *what are you cooking?* Don't know – *lets see what you've got* – [freezer opened to show a weeks supply of individual frozen convenience foods] – we do it in the oven. *How do you decide what you're going to eat?* – We can eat anything – *I know, I can see it there – but how do you decide what to have?* I do the cooking today.

Do you get on well with the other two? Yes. *Do you get lonely here on your own when they go out?* It's all right. *At Wentwood you had lots of people – did you like that better?* Yes. *Did you all come here together?* Yes. *Was it very strange in the beginning?* It was all right. *Did some one live in in the beginning?* Yes – but nobody lives in now? No.

Yet you think that it was better at Wentwood than here? Yes. *Can you tell me why?* I don't know. *What did you do there that was different?* It was better.

Would you like to go back to Wentwood if you could? Yes, I want to go back. *What would you do if you went back?* I had my friends there, had friends there.

Would you like to live with your Mum? Yep. *Would you like to live with your Dad?* Sometimes I'd like to.

You're very independent aren't you – er – do you know what independent means, it means you do things all by yourself. Yep. *Do you like living here?* Not a lot of the time – I like it better at Wentwood.

You don't like this group home? Not all the time no. *Why not?* Everyone is rowing. *What are they rowing about –* having coffee at night. *Was the food better at Wentwood –* better yes, and there were jobs to do –

Haven't you got all those things here…

[Tears. Quite unexpectedly Gillian, who had been happily laughing her way through the interview put her head in her hands and cried quietly and hopelessly.]

You don't like thinking about here do you? No. *Would you like to go on somewhere else from here or are you quite happy here?* I can't stay. *You can't stay – why not?* I want to go back to Wentwood.

Wentwood is for younger people than you – it's like a school and you're too old and independent for school now; would you like to go to another home where Mrs Reynolds was? Yes.

Aren't you happy here? No, I'm not very happy here, there are arguments here. *What about?* Who does the cooking – Mary all the time. *She wants to do the cooking?* Yes – *but you have a list who does the cooking – would you like to do more cooking?* Yes – *and she doesn't let you?* No.

Which of you argues the most? Mary. *Ann seems ever so nice* – Yes she is. *Mary isn't so nice?* No not all the time. I don't like her.

What does Mary do that you don't like? She's not nice. *Do you like her boyfriend?* Not all the time. *Would you like it if he didn't come* – no – *you don't mind him?* I mind him a lot.

Why, is he silly some of time? A bit silly – *what does he do when he's a bit silly?* Silly swearing some of the time – *You don't like that?* No. *You don't like swear words?* No. *Who does he swear at?* Mary – *not you* – no. That's all right so long as he's swearing at Mary not you [Gillian laughs].

If you could choose how would you like to live? At Wentwood. *Would you like to live on your own all by yourself –in a house like this all by yourself?* Yes

Does your Mum live by herself? Yes – *and you'd like to live by yourself like that. Could you manage* – yep. *Would you like to live in a bigger house with more people, so you'd have more friends?* Yes more friends,

Do you remember being at Wentwood? Yes. *Do you like it better here or better at Wentwood [long silence] – which is better?* Hard. *Where would you like to be here or Wentwood?* I'd rather be at Wentwood yes.

What was good about it? I got jobs all right. *Where did you do jobs?* Sometimes we had hobbies – *and did you do any work experience in Wentwood?* Yes. *What did you do?* Painting on the wall. *Would you like to go back to Wentwood?* I do yes.

Do you the three of you ever go out together – no – *what do you do at nights* – stay in – *Do you go to any centres or anything?* No

Do you like the people that help you here like Alice? Yes. *But you'd still rather be with more friends like you were at Wentwood?* Yes. *Have you got friends at the other places you go?* Yes – yes a lot of friends – *and have you got friends at work?* Yes I've got friends.

Do you ever go to the pub? Yes I go Friday to the pub with my Dad – we go to bingo Friday. *Does he come every Friday?* He picks me up.

Do you go to church? Yes Sundays. *Do you go to church every Sunday?* Yes, I go on my own down the road. *Do you all go?* No only one go, me. *Do you like the church?* Yea I do. *What time do you go to church?* I got to set off quarter to eleven.

Have you been confirmed? Yes. *Did you get confirmed at Wentwood?* Yes. *Why do you go every Sunday, have you always gone?* Yep. *Did you have harvest festival?* Yes last week. *Did you take anything?* Yes potatoes. *Where did you put the potatoes?* In the bag – *yes but where did you put them in the church?* On the table.

Is church one of the best things you do? Yes, I go to Bible class. *What do you do in Bible class?* We sing songs. *Do the other two go?* No only me. *How do you get there?* A keyworker takes me there. *What time does it finish?* Half past nine.

What do you do – can you show me any of it? [Produces a child's prayer and drawing book] *Did you do that?* Yes – *Can you read this* – I can read – *what's it about* – about Christ. *Do you follow Jesus* – yes –

[We look through book and she reads odd words with no understanding of the text.]

'The world and all that's in it belongs to the Lord' *what does that mean* – [long pause] – don't know. *Do you say your prayers at night?* The Lord watch over those who trust Him verse 18. *How many people go* – a lot of people – *who do you sit with* – on my own.

Social worker

She does very well really. Life's difficult for all of us. When she was first coming she visited and came and stayed here and then she decided to move in. Gillian organises her own life, that's how we operate here. All three ladies have a different calendar and they or we write down where they're going, write it down here on the wall.

We have several small pilot project houses on the estate. I come in once a week to sort the money out – they need a little help budgeting for the week. They do have rent to pay – we take that off for them. Someone else comes in to help her wash and help her with her personal appearance and bath. That's agreed with Gillian. We can't help – we're social services and we can't do personal care – it's not part of our brief. On Monday evening she attends a 'look good – feel good' workshop. We're very fortunate, most of the clients who attend our workshops can travel on public transport but all three have a taxi for that. I do this class where they learn to look after their face and put lotions on. They have worksheets for this, and health, and money, and shopping lists.

[Produces a variety of excellent lists which are clear and well thought out]

They have their ups and downs and don't always agree. Now if somebody's coming they're not happy about they'll have a house meeting. I do these now. We had a lady who came on a Thursday and they didn't particularly like her – so we had a discussion and now she doesn't come. That's what we'll do – we'll have a discussion.

We have three projects in this area. I support two other ladies who live totally independently in their own houses and two gentleman who live independently.

Who is James that Gillian says comes here?

James lives in the group home that I support. He sometimes comes up to see you – sometimes you have to chase him away cause he's a pest isn't he Gillian?

(GILLIAN: **He's a pain in the arse.**)

Mother

Her mother confirmed everything that Gillian had said about the complexities of her daily routine and the different places she went to. How she got there was accurate – even down to the correct taxi and bus fares. It appeared that Gillian had given a surprisingly coherent and detailed account of her life.

Do you think that Wentwood did a lot for Gillian? Yes I think they had quite a tough time with her – *the records show good progress –*

There are areas in which she is not at all strong and they did a vast amount of work on her in those areas when she was at Wentwood and it didn't stick. To do with her personal appearance and care, keeping clean and tidy and well presented. She would always put her clothes on back to front and inside out.

She looked very nice when I saw her –

That's partly because she has someone from the community team to help with those things because I got really worried about it. She became incontinent and was getting fatter and fatter and fatter – in desperation I asked if she could have some extra help. The incontinence has only happened over the last six months and I was afraid it was to do with her weight and not being able to control her muscles. In fact it was some sort of urinary infection which cleared up. She was incontinent for a long time. She had been occasionally in the car – or occasionally in the sitting room here. It distressed her a lot – she really hated it. Every time I went in I found that she she had a wet bed and her mattress was wet. We had to get a rainwater type mattress and waterproof cover for her duvet.

The team are good are they?

> Yes – they've got two different agencies in there. They've got the Health Authority who are nurses, a welfare assistant and an occupational therapist and then you've got Social Services. Its the first time that the Community Team have ever been involved in a group home and they were rather pleased to be asked in. There's a little bit of you know – 'do they do what they are supposed to do and why are they leaving it for me to do etc!'

One of the remarks surprised me with one keyworker – she said she was a rehab officer and that was one of the things she couldn't do. I think they are having a few problems sorting it out.

Did Wentwood improve Gillian? Enormously. *Was that maintained then?*

> No that's the trouble, we all make mistakes and I think perhaps I'm more responsible for it than anybody. She went straight from Wentwood into the group home without any sort of easing her in. That was what she wanted to do, she didn't want to come home and live with me. I ought to have known because in the holidays she used to come home and she'd have a beautiful plan of what she was going to do in the holidays from Wentwood. In quite small detail and for two or three mornings she'd do that beautifully. After that she reverted to her sort of behaviour that she was doing before she went to Wentwood and if not hounded she'd stay in bed all day.

She told me she was happier at Wentwood than she is here. She said she'd like to go back to Wentwood. I'm sure she would.

She said she was very happy there with lots to do and lots of friends. I think she'd never been in a situation where there wasn't somebody in charge on the premises.

Are you happy with her there or would you prefer her somewhere more structured?

> I'm quite happy with her there but I'd like her to go to MacIntyre [A local charitable structured working community for people with learning disabilities]. I wouldn't like Gillian to go out of the area because her father and I live very close. She was trained by the day centre here and they followed by car to see she caught the right buses.

She was trained at Wentwood too.

> Yes, she came home by coach by herself – but it only occurred occasionally so it didn't stick. Henrietta would follow her round Bath and dodge behind pillars to see what she was up to and Gillian was sitting on the floor emptying her bag to find something – literally on the ground and some unsavoury-looking character was coming up to ask if he could

help her and Henrietta felt it was time for her to intervene. Now she goes to work on the bus and she has to change buses.

I was impressed with the niceness of the people in the house, although Gillian says they aren't – and the ease with which I was welcomed and the nice feeling about the place. She took me out shopping after the others had gone out. She bought two lunches for today and tomorrow and she counted the right money out. She bought two pork pies, two packets of crisps and two egg sandwiches. It was £3.59 and she counted out £3 and looked at the till and found some change. The woman was very nice and waited till she had everything – a few people in the queue had to wait but they didn't seem to mind.

She was actually mugged outside that shop. She wouldn't tell you that. She got mugged about nine months ago. She just went in to get her allowances on her own and she put the money in her bag because she was told very definitely that she must do that but the lads who mugged her just took the whole thing out of her hand. They took the money and and threw the bag on the ground.

Was anybody watching? I don't know. *But its only across the road, she can be seen from the houses there.* It's not opposite – *it's not far* – its not far but its far enough. *Was she very upset about it?*

Yes, and the others have been. They called the police and now they're not allowed to go on their own. They go in twos or all together. The others have been stopped and asked for money and cigarettes but that's life on an estate I'm afraid. She was also found in the sitting room with the door open and the housekeeping money gone. When asked whether the door was locked she said it was.

Did she let them in? No. *How did they get in?*

They got in with a big stick. I think that she went to the door and opened it. She's not doing that now.

She is! I was bothered, there is a chain but there was no chain on the door, which bothered me. The council bloke came in with his strimmer to cut the lawn and he had to walk right through the house to the back. It's fair enough, as the council have a contract and there is no other way to the back garden but he could have been anybody. There was no chain on the door. I asked about the chain and she said she did it at night but I wasn't happy about that. She knew him and he knew her but he could have been anybody. So there is one level where this independence is not so good?

That's right. The other two are quite a lot older than her and they're more experienced at being in the community and that's helped her a lot. I don't think she'd have gone in unless she had gone in with people who had a little more know-how than her. Her morale may be good now but after all she's been there four or five years.

Are you happy with her there?

Yes, I'm very happy with her there. I like knowing what's going on and the more the rehab team can involve me in what they are doing and what's going on, the happier I am about it. I work in the hospital and if any of them need anything in the house I can sort it out. It seems ideal on one level – I don't know if it would be if it were just Gillian.

They seem to eat a lot of convenience food – they had ham and an occasional frozen chop – but mostly cooking seemed to be reheating three separate packs of convenience food.

Yes, it's difficult, there's no fresh meat in the shop. I'm nearing retirement age and I was thinking that is something I could do with them, teaching them proper cooking. They have done it, they've all done it but you know what it's like when you go to a cookery class – everything is there and you follow instructions with cook in charge with big ovens and big fridges. I would like to do it on a much smaller level. Going to the shops to buy something to cook and bringing it home. I think from time to time the rehab team have tried to, but they really haven't got the manpower to do it.

Gillian's weight is one of the worst problems. When she left Wentwood she weighed 9 stone – she now weighs 13. Her dislocation of the hip wasn't diagnosed until she was eight. She was looked over by the paediatrician – but Down's babies have very loose joints and she didn't walk till she was five.

Gillian reads, but there again, at school we were told quite definitely that reading was not on the curriculum and I was led to believe that it was something she would not be able to do.

She can write well. She wrote all the phone numbers and addresses down for me.
Oh yes – for the record it was not the school that taught her, it was me.

We went into the supermarket and she picked up some new vegetarian things she hadn't seen been before from the freezer – quite complicated mushroom something and cauliflower something – and she said what are these? So I said – what are they? She read them without any problems.

Both my husband and I have always been extremely keen for her to live in the community and not be segregated – we're really quite sort of political about that. When I say to people that Social Services are extremely constructive and very good, people say – well they saw you coming!

I am very happy that the welfare worker is going in because she does keep an eye on Gillian's hygiene and clothes. She's bought a lot of clothes.

She says she chooses them with the staff and not with you. That's right, its something that Alice has taken on.

She takes her to Bible class. Its impressive the number of places she goes to. Yes, I take her out and she knows everybody – people actually warm to her. I can see that you've warmed to her.

I wonder why she would rather go back to Wentwood and that she would rather not live there?

When she came back from Wentwood and before we had really bad trouble about her settling in, you'd talk about Wentwood and she'd say – I want to do my own thing – I want to do it all myself.

That's what they were taught at Wentwood, that the normal thing was to get away from home and live on your own.

I have them all here to lunch on Sunday. *You take them all to the cinema.* They have to pay. *Have any of the others got a family?* They don't seem to have much family at all.

I usually take her away in the summer. She goes camping with her father. One of his sidelines is a book business and if he has a book fair he takes Gillian and he leaves her in charge and goes off to talk to other people – and if people give her money they usually take the change. People at book fairs are quite nice. She goes telling at election times – she goes and sits outside the booth and people give her their cards. I'm dangling a carrot – if she manages to get down to 12 stone we'll go to Eurodisney but its not very likely.

If I'm away and my husband finds it very difficult to have her where he is, she goes into a hostel. If I'm away at Easter time she goes into the hostel for respite care.

Does she mind? She loves it. She loves the more people being around the better. *She said to me she'd like more friends – do you think she'd be happier in a larger place?*

I don't know. It seems such a step ahead to be in a small group home rather than a hostel that I'm rather loathe to backtrack. But I would have thought that she would have rather preferred and have had more enjoyment going to the day centre which is next to the hostel. She went there originally before all these people became involved.

Did she like it?

She loves to have all the people around.

Then why doesn't she go?

> Because everybody thinks its better for her to get on two buses and
> we've fussed for her to go to work and all the rest of it, you see. But the
> others go to the day centres. We've fought for it, as it were, and now
> we're stuck with it. I remember saying quite recently why don't we
> listen to what Gillian is saying. Self-advocacy and all that stuff. Gillian's
> saying that she wants to go and work at the day centre. Why can't we
> let her do that?

She said to me that she wants to do that, or she wants to go back to Wentwood
where she had lots of friends and jobs to do, yet really her life style is very impressive.

> I think if she went to the hostel she would just sink into the comfortable
> routine of it. The warden being there. You lose if they are segregated,
> you lose the contact with the community and the independence. Basi-
> cally she's doing all the things in the community that she would be
> doing in the centre – with the same people when you think about it.

She really does beg the question of what we should we do – because she does so well.
What ideally have you thought you want for Gillian?

> I'm torn. Actually I think I would like her to to go to MacIntyre really
> but its a question of funding. It's realistic at MacIntyre, they work and
> they market what they work – its on an ordinary city estate – with flats
> and a place for care-staff separately. Gillian works in the selling part of
> the nursery which has a bakery and the plants. She knows all the people
> there but it costs such a lot of money and the council won't pay.
>
> If I said I wanted Gillian to go to a residential home which is what
> MackIntyre would be – they'd say we've got Gillian in our group home
> and that's OK. When she first came home it wasn't any different. I can
> understand their point of view. There are children with severe behav-
> iour problems with nowhere to go – but they're the sort of people that
> get the special provisions. Whether we want it now – we've got it, but
> now we've got it it's a different matter.

She does seem to have a very full life – really she's achieved the blueprint – an
ordinary life.

> But whether the blueprint is what we really want we'll never know.
> Who drew up the blueprint?

CHAPTER 6

Overview

The usual conclusions to a research project have been pre-empted by the protagonists in this study. Throughout the text, parents, staff and ex-students have given their individual conclusions that challenge many of the current assumptions and provisions of care in the community for people with learning disabilities.

It is difficult to equate the printed transcriptions of the interviews with the information that the general IQ range of the ex-student sample was between 30 and 46. Auditory and visual impressions gained when visiting people left no ambiguity as to their clinical syndromes and associated physical disabilities. Even those people who might have have been assumed to be more able manifested their disability by their speed of response or slow and indistinct speech.

The research looked at three more or less equal groups of ex-students, comprised of people living in the family home, in staffed group homes or independently with non-residential support staff. As shown throughout the text, skill gains and losses also reflected these living environments. All the ex-students remaining in the family home lost skills, and consequent independence, through lack of practice. Post-Wentwood, people living in group homes and independent provisions continued to gain skills in their new environments. It had been assumed that those students with the highest ex-Wentwood final assessment would be found to be happily settled in the more independent provisions. The results of the research did not support this view nor did the interviews with the ex-students. A high proportion of the most successful and independent students were unhappy in their community settings.

All the interviews highlighted an unexpected on-going emotional dependency which has not yet been fully recognised in the provision of care in the community for this group of people. A surprising finding, running throughout the text, was the insistence of people living in group homes or independent provisions with minimal support to regard everyone in authority as 'staff' – even when their contact with them was limited to a couple of hours a week. They seemed to derive continuing emotional support from these 'staff' and used this term when talking about them rather than using people's names. There was no indication of any previous institutionalisation in the sample as, for most of them, Wentwood was the first time they had left the family home. Clearly demonstrated in the text is the desire of some people, successfully living in the more independent community provisions, to return to a more dependent communal life style. They are now asking for staff to help direct their social and working lives. At their own request they are giving up their hard earned independence and trying to find places in sheltered communities where they will be assured of meaningful work opportunities and a full social life with their peers.

OCCUPATION

Most independent group homes and private family placements would only accept people if local authority daytime sheltered occupation, with transport, was available. The brochures of these homes indicated that residential places would only be offered against such a daytime placement. This would appear to discriminate against people who could otherwise have held Youth Training or other jobs within the local community. There was a bias towards the Adult Training Centre (or equivalent), rather than a College of Education, due to the overlong holidays in educational provisions which would mean that more daytime staff cover would be needed in the group home. In mitigation, part-time Further Education placements were often organised through the Adult Centre which either allowed the student to travel independently or provided the necessary transport. Once at the college some students had been offered various types of Youth Training placements consisting of half a day or a day a week. Post-Wentwood, all leavers had managed to attend some form of Further Education.

There appeared to be different attitudes towards men and women by parents and professionals with regard to occupational opportunities. Many of the women had done voluntary work at some time, and were still doing so, mainly in play groups and old people's homes. Only one man had done any voluntary work at any time since leaving Wentwood.

WORK

People had left Wentwood with a clear expectation that work was to be part of their daily life. As shown in the text, 52 per cent of the ex-students held full or part-time jobs in their local community alongside their 'able' workmates. ten per cent had held similar jobs but had left them for various reasons – which did not include being asked to leave. In common with others in their age group, government Youth Training Schemes accounted for many of the jobs. The majority travelled to work independently on public transport and, despite their limited intellect, appeared to understand the implications of the work and had little difficulty completing it to their employers' satisfaction. These figures represent a substantial achievement in the current economic climate of high unemployment. Firms such as McDonald's who have a clear national policy on the employment of people with disabilities have contributed to a change of outlook by employers.

The ethics of payment for such work is beyond the scope of this research, but as shown in the text, the general opinion of parents, staff and workers was that the self-esteem gained by the worker outweighed the financial considerations. There seemed to be a recognition that the worker would generally work rather more slowly than the majority of the workforce – except Lizzie, the least able of the ex-students, whose case study shows that her skills and speed exceeded those of her workmates!

There seemed to be no explanation for ability of a high proportion of the sample who were able to hold down jobs for several years in their local communities. The only common denominator in this group, regardless of other abilities, was that in the majority of cases assessment on the Gunzburg P-A-C2 Mobility section showed a subscore of three skills or above. This appeared to be a necessary pre-requisite for work in the wider community indicating that people would be capable of independent travel to and from work. It would seem that if people were unable to get themselves to work and back, it was unlikely that anyone else would be able to do so on a daily basis – either in the community or the parental home. Evidence throughout the text shows that where a person achieved this level, family, keyworkers and staff would help them practice a particular journey until they were competent to travel independently. Parents were unanimous in their belief that without the experience of the concentrated Wentwood travel curriculum (by foot, bike, bus and train) they would not have contemplated the idea of independent travel for their sons and daughters. However, such skills in themselves do not usually form an adequate explanation of continuing stability of employment.

ASSESSMENT

As shown throughout the text, the main area of inadequacy by professionals towards people with learning disabilities, regardless of the type of living environment, was that of assessment. People living in twos and threes in the small houses in the community that now constitute group homes lived with differing degrees of support. As seen in Gillian's case study, several agencies were often concerned with the welfare of a single individual. They range through social service keyworkers, care assistants, voluntary workers, and in the case of people with minor physical disabilities, representatives from the Area Health Authority. There was little contact between the groups. These new community provisions seem to be fragmented and quite unrelated to the staffing structure of the larger institutions which have a tradition of record keeping and assessment.

Parents recognised that people living in the family home were at a distinct disadvantage but felt unable to do anything about this. They had all lost a substantial number of life skills and many were now no longer capable of living a semi-independent life. There seemed to be no clear definition of the keyworkers role vis-à-vis parents. The tendency for keyworkers to meet these clients away from the family home, combined with the lack of knowledge by parents of the role of the keyworker, makes on-going assessment and the consequent recognition of these lost skills in the family home unlikely. The current emphasis on a search for assessment methodology, rather than doing the assessment, seems unhelpful. Sadly, it is unlikely that any clear assessment guidelines (such as those used nationally by Health Visitors when assessing young children in the family home or clinic) will be found. Even the assessments with which people arrived at a home were often disregarded, as staff could not equate them with those in use in the new environment. Assessment is time consuming. Because of current economic stringencies and staff shortages assessment is usually found to be too time consuming. On a simple level, either people can do things or they can't, and only some form of assessment will establish what a person can do and whether opportunities to practise relevant life skills are available in their environment. Without ongoing assessment people with learning disabilities usually regress and are unable realise their full potential.

QUALITY OF LIFE

Ffity-five per cent thought that, on balance, their current lifestyle was better than the Wentwood lifestyle, but still cited many factors of the Wentwood experience that they wished they could still do. People in group homes had fewer complaints than the other two groups and of these only one person decided life was worse now. The feelings of isolation and boredom experienced by people in the family home and those living more independent lives in the community were not reported by people living in group homes.

Seventeen per cent of the ex-students considered their current lifestyle was worse than that they had enjoyed at Wentwood. Others cited many negative aspects but were not prepared to give either a negative or affirmative reply. There were clear indications that for many of the ex-students their current lifestyle was considerably more restrictive and emotionally barren than it had been at Wentwood.

More women than men thought their life was not as good as it had been in Wentwood. Interviews with parents, staff and ex-students revealed that many women felt the loss of Wentwood because they were now more sheltered than men by every agency. National concern over the murder of a relatively independent female ex-student (with Down's Syndrome) on her way home from a local Leisure Centre could well have been a contributory factor. Many parents with sons and daughters living at home preferred the local authority provision of sheltered occupation, and its attendant transport provisions, to other more independent options.

People with Down's Syndrome complained of finding life in the community physically demanding, too noisy and too rushed. Some of them had given up a variety of work experience or voluntary placements for this reason. 'Too much' was a syndrome-specific complaint. Evidence was found of a developmental difference in ageing between young adults with Down's syndrome and the rest of the sample. The women in particular clearly and succinctly expressed their discomfort within the work environment, town centres, busy supermarkets and even the adult training centre. The author was not surprised at this finding. As far back as 1971 an attempt to validate the Progress Assessment Chart 1 on 200 children with Down's syndrome aged 6–15 years led to a new developmental arrangement of the original P-A-C which then became a separate assessment chart relating to Down's syndrome. The original P-A-C had been standardised on a group of children and adolescents with differing clinical syndromes including Down's syndrome (Gunzburg and Sinson 1974).

For the majority of the ex-students, wherever they were living, their only peer contact was with people of similar ability. Their social life was in clubs for people with learning disabilities such as Gateway, as were their holidays. As shown in Chapter 3, people with jobs were the only people with learning disabilities in their workplace. Sadly they appeared to be unable to make friends or have anything other than very superficial contact with their workmates. However, the 12 per cent who had only 'able' friends and refused to take part in any social events for people like themselves were cut off from most of the available opportunities for social life. This resulted in the feelings of alienation and the subsequent family stress shown in Chapter 4.

Set against the disadvantages of living at home was the fact that parents were prepared to provide a varied social life, holidays and many extras not so easily available to the other two groups. People in the other two groups were often unable to have holidays or pursue expensive hobbies due to lack of money. This was particularly true for residents in religious foundations who provided an outstanding level of care in every other respect. The children of high income families living away from home suffered similar financial stringencies to those from lower income families. Several of such offspring proudly showed photographs of the family boat and holiday home etc., whilst not having had a holiday themselves for two years. Interviews with parents failed to reveal any particular reason for this anomaly and staff who recognised this phenomenen offered the differing explanations shown in the text.

For many people church and church activities were an important part of their lives. For most people, the local church was within walking distance and people from all three living groups often went to church on their own. This was so even when their families or other group home residents were non-attenders. People attended Bible reading classes and many church social functions and for the majority of people the church provided the only social contact, outside the immediate family, with other adult members of the local community. Where religious provisions were part of the living unit and extended to holidays, outings and clubs, peoples lives were enriched. One particular foundation which existed to bring together families of people with learning disabilities as well as providing group homes, extended a much appreciated invitation to their prayer meetings and other activities to people with learning disabilities and their families living in the community. The proportion of churchgoers could have been unusually high as three of the group homes were funded by religious bodies. However, previous projects by the author showed a similar finding with regard to church attendance.

Positive values carried over from Wentwood coloured the ex-student interviews. The two main expectations after leaving Wentwood had been the opportunity to work and the enjoyment of communal life with all its attendant leisure opportunities. In retrospect, there seemed little point in learning to live an independent life and to be proficient in leisure activities such as sport and gardening if, subsequently, there was no-one with whom to share these skills.

Appendix

Wentwood[1]

Henrietta Reynolds (HR) established Wentwood Education in 1980 and subsequently worked there for the next decade. She set out to prove that an intensive residential pre-vocational course would give the young adult with special needs the ability and confidence to live an independent life within the community. It was also envisaged that this particular approach would extend the students' horizons beyond the somewhat restrictive world of the ATC. Wanting to control, and if possible eliminate, the overprotective background often experienced by students leaving special schools when they try to enter an adult world of growing independence, she decided that a residential setting was the most appropriate for her students. The intake was to be restricted to those students who were transferring from the then named ESN/S (educationally subnormal/severe) schools, or those within a similar IQ range from other sources. Thus the records analysed were from students with recorded IQ scores of below 55 or equivalent mental ages.

The material, which charts the development of young adults with severe learning disabilities through an intensive two-year residential social education course, was not originally collected for the purpose of research. However, it was possible to approach a subsequent research project with the confidence of reliability, as during the decade 1980–90 meticulous records and P-A-C assessments had been kept on all the students entering this private sixth-form college. The curriculum, teaching methods and assessments were based on P-A-C methodology. The students completed the two year course with regular six-monthly assessments, because of this it was also possible to use the records of the entire student intake over the ten years, without any strategic pruning of results. The only records not used were those for the handful of students who for various reasons did not complete the two year course and those students who had not completed the course by May 1990. Thus it was possible to establish a base line for every student graduating over the ten years, and so define progress from admission to departure.

As Wentwood is a private concern, combining residential training of life skills with a clear educational component, the cost of staffing such a college with a high staff/student ratio is unusually high. In the light of the current financial stringencies in the public sector, if the Wentwood method, and results can be seen to effectively equip the young adult with special needs to cope with policies of community integration, then it should be regarded to be ultimately cost effective. Almost certainly the controversy about the desirability and feasibility of such schemes will continue throughout the next decade. It may well be that a closer consideration of this particular forward-looking undertaking may add some positive elements to the

---

1 Reprinted from Sinson 1993 *Group Homes and Community Integration and Developmentally Disabled People: Micro-Institutionalisation.*

debate. One indication of the success of Wentwood is suggested by the fact that the majority of students over the past three years have managed to achieve a measure of self-sufficiency. Most of them are living relatively independent lives in small community houses (with varying degrees of staff dependence) rather than in hospitals, larger group homes or with their families.

THE ENVIRONMENT

The initial difficulties of finding suitable accommodation for Wentwood involved rejecting many different geographical locations. For the P-A-C training programme to be effective, students had to live both within a well-defined urban community and yet be sufficiently distanced from amenities. This would enable the training programme to be designed with realistic graduated progression and challenges. Effective transport links were essential to enable parents to visit easily and for students to be taught to travel home independently for holidays and short visits. A range of sporting facilities were required within the locality to enable students to experience the same choice of independent leisure activities as their more fortunate siblings. A large garden with outbuildings was necessary to develop those often tedious occupations of gardening and house maintenance which are usually substituted by contract provisions in local authority residential group homes.

Eventually such a location was found, comprising a large nineteenth-century rectory set in the original village square and adjoining the church and vicarage, around which a small market town had developed. There was extensive ribbon development leading to factories, housing estates, motorways, sports centre and all the impedimenta of twentieth-century urban life. Two years later the adjoining vicarage, the Grove, was acquired to enable seven students to spend the final part of their course living almost fully independent lives with a minimum of staff supervision.

THE STUDENTS

Ninety students have attended Wentwood over the decade including those still completing their course. Their ages on departure ranged from 17 to 22 years. The majority of students have local authority backing with the main catchment area being adjoining authorities in the south of England. The social class distribution was broadly that found in the normal population with a slightly higher proportion of middle class students from the more geographically distant locations. This was not Wentwood policy, but was assumed to have arisen through the ability of articulate middle-class parents to persuade the funding authorities to co-operate in Further Education projects. Such parents also had a more ready acceptance of boarding school and college life. All the students were ambulant, although several had both sensory and minor physical disabilities, and were within the 40–55 IQ range.

Intending students had to spend a trial period of assessment at the college. The students who were not accepted at the end of this two-week trial were those students who appeared over sophisticated and already competent in some of the personal and social skills needed for both leisure and work. It was felt that, although currently attending special schools, they would feel understretched by the Wentwood curriculum which was designed for the more severely disabled adolescent. Students were never rejected because they had too few skills, but some students were turned down due to their physical disabilities requiring more space than was available in the domestic setting of the college.

THE STAFF

Fourteen members of staff were employed which gave a staff/student ratio of one member of staff to four students during the day. This ratio decreased during evenings and weekends, to two staff in the main house for twelve students and one in the annexe for the seven more independent students. This decrease during the students' leisure time resulted in students in both houses having to cope with areas of their daily life with very little supervision. This was a deliberate and planned policy. Because there were no domestic or maintenance staff, this so-called leisure time was filled with the sort of domestic and personal tasks that would have normally required staff supervision or have been performed by domestic staff in local authority group homes.

Staff were employed both to teach a special subject and to be a general member of staff. The policy was for each member of staff to wear a different 'hat', with their special subject title drawn from the P-A-C section headings. For example, an individual member of staff was responsible for each of the main P-A-C areas of Self-help, Communication, Socialisation and Occupation. Within these confines, different staff members had a responsibility for the more specialised subsections. For example, 'travel' taught by HR was a subsection termed Mobility within in the P-A-C Self-help sector. This led to a novel approach to the curriculum, in that when staff were on duty, the lessons the students had during that period reflected the 'hat' of the teacher. As all teachers did equal time on the rota and students worked in small groups of four, this became a very effective way of teaching. The staff rota dominated the curriculum and as their duty time included a selection of day, overnight and weekend periods, this ensured that effective teaching went on throughout almost every minute of the students' waking day. Each teacher also had an equal amount of day rota time for formal academic-type group teaching. Not only did each member of staff have to teach a special subject in the P-A-C area but they were also responsible for making small-step teaching breakdowns for each skill in their P-A-C area. They were expected to record and inform every other member of staff, on a daily basis, of each student's progress and level of achievement in their own area. This enabled staff on duty at other times to decide which students they could send shopping with £10.00 in their purse and which students they had to stretch to count the pennies – and similar decisions. As they all needed money every day for bus fares, shopping, sports centre and the like, the result of such an integrated curriculum was that not only financial dealings, but all other areas of the curriculum, were applied both in the classroom and wherever they were a part of everyday life. An important result of this type of staff unity was that no time was wasted by a teacher sending a student off to do a task below their ability. Consequently, students' abilities were permanently stretched.

Weekly staff meetings were held. Alternative staff were employed to work with the students during this time to enable all staff to both attend the meetings and to have a break from teaching. Two students were discussed each week in the staff meeting. The discussion focused on an assessment form which had been left out all the previous week, for each student. Every member of staff had to complete their own subject listing current progress, achievements and immediate goals. HR insisted that there was no room in a well-run curriculum for woolly thinking or the concept of staff all 'mucking in together'. She felt that her approach to staff accountability, with its meticulous recording and assessment procedures, although generating a large amount of paperwork, was in the best interests of her students.

The effect of such careful attention to detail was to ensure that every member of staff had access to all relevant information about each student. This was often pinned behind doors or otherwise strategically concealed in kitchens, bedrooms, bathrooms etc and reflected the current ability and immediate goals of each student in that particular social skill area. One of the main objectives of this type of procedure, in relation to the staff, was to ensure that every member of staff was involved in realistic follow up teaching in every P-A-C area. A typical example is students who were unable (or unwilling) to wipe their own bottom. This information was up on the wall in the toilets and all staff were requested to go to the toilet with certain students whatever they were teaching. Many teachers find the concept of being employed to teach a special subject, such as gardening or communication skills, and also to be responsible for the toileting of an adult student, an appalling concept. This type of procedure required both the most intense communication between all members of staff and also relied on the absolute necessity of all staff carrying out this procedure. If a student went to the toilet five times a day his own way, but was only supervised at bedtimes, he was not going to learn. If however, every time he went to the toilet every member of staff, both male and female, applied the same rules, then the student would eventually learn.

No student was ever allowed by any member of staff to do any task incorrectly. Contrary to much of today's educational practice, Wentwood staff did not believe in students learning from their own mistakes, but that the correct habits must be instilled and constantly repeated from the very beginning of the learning process.

EVOLVING A CURRICULUM

The curriculum was designed to incorporate basic scientific learning principles into every-day living so that social skills would be meaningfully acquired. It was also realised that one of the salient features of such a programme was the assessment of each student at regular intervals, so that both progress and regression could be carefully monitored from a previously obtained base line. This information was then fed back into the teaching programme. This base line would enable Wentwood to recognise any basic social skills that were either missing or very weak, in each individual student, at the start of the course. Also to establish whether these were due to lack of previous opportunity or genuine inability. It was hoped the final assessment would measure both the student's progress and the effectiveness of the two-year teaching programme. Because life at Wentwood was based on the P-A-C recording system for social and personal development, it was possible to design an entire curriculum on this diagnostic tool. This initiated standard assessment procedure from which the curriculum would be evolved. To this end, it was particularly important to site the students in an environment which would enable them to experience all the relevant independent life skills as a regular part of their day. This would facilitate a continuity of approach for both teaching and assessment methodology.

As Wentwood was a pre-vocational course, emphasis was only placed on those academic skills that were directly relevant to social and independent living. By using the P-A-C developmental approach, based on standardised well-documented levels of attainment, six-monthly regular assessments enabled each student to be taught to maximise key developmental skills at the appropriate time in conjunction with other relevant social skills. A unique feature of the unified curriculum which finally evolved was this use of *assessment as the starting point of the curriculum* rather than the more usual random fragmented procedure found in most training schemes involving young adults with learning difficulties.

Parents were asked to continue certain learning programmes in the holidays, usually concentrating on leisure activities from the P-A-C areas. This not only gave parents positive objectives to aim for, but also introduced them to the concept of assessment. Many letters from parents, to be found in the students' records, outlined holiday successes could almost have been direct quotations from the P-A-C manual.

The P-A-C method was not designed to provide a comprehensive curriculum in a strict academic sense but to provide the individual with at least the minimum amount of social knowledge necessary to live a reasonably independent life in the immediate environment. However the Wentwood approach extended the method into an effective curriculum. Recognising that the P-A-C analysis of skills was to be the starting point HR realised that the scoring criteria and breakdown of skills was not detailed enough to serve as a teaching method. Over time, she and other Wentwood staff examined each skill and produced detailed breakdowns to enable teaching to proceed in logical graduated steps. These were incorporated into the curriculum to be used by all staff with each student. On the simplest level, there were 28 steps identified when students learn to clean their teeth including the use of excluding tablets so that students can see what they were cleaning. A far more complex road safety and travel programme was used by more advanced students. All kitchen skills were illustrated with simple stage by stage pictorial diagrams displayed on the wall alongside cookers and kettles etc often illustrating negative procedure with a cross through the incorrect picture. This ensures that students always have a quick reference point when working on their own.

A singular feature of the Wentwood way of life is the incorporation of these carefully designed procedural programmes into every aspect of the students' daily life, with relevant programmes displayed on walls and checkcards in every room in the house. Students always followed each step of every teaching programme in the correct context. In the early stages of training no attempt was made to either generalise or transfer aspects of training to any other skill. The author had personal experience as to the efficacy of one of the domestic training programmes and consistency of staff approach. On her first visit to Wentwood the staff on breakfast duty were called away to an urgent problem. The group of students who were detailed to clear and clean the dining room seemed unsure what to do. It transpired that one had only arrived the previous night and the others were relatively new to the rota. Picking up one of the many checkcards in the room, she found it possible for a complete stranger to implement the procedure and enable the students to work through the rota and finish in time to attend their morning meeting as usual.

Since 1950 philosophy and research in the field of mental retardation has concentrated on the rights and the abilities of people with learning disabilities to make individual and meaningful choices in their daily life. This ethos is particularly prevalent in the current swing away from institutional life and the concept of community integration. The Wentwood philosophy, by initially placing the student in a rigidly controlled environment, with little or no choice allowed in any aspect of daily life, would seem to be a negation of these principles. Yet the ultimate aim of the Wentwood two-year course is to enable each person to realise their full potential for independent living.

IMPLEMENTING THE CURRICULUM FOR LEISURE

The curriculum provides an intensely active day which challenges a students' physical and mental resources. The hope is that this will also break the more usual lethargic dependent lifestyle of the adult with developmental disabilities and encourage the use of leisure time in a more personally beneficial way.

Surprisingly, for such a innovative college, the Wentwood day would be easily recognisable by anyone who had spent their formative years as a boarder in a British public school. The student's day starts very early at seven o'clock and finishes equally early. All students attend the nine o'clock morning meeting where the day's activities are discussed and any student problems are sorted out by the member of staff detailed for that day. Students also give brief reports on varying activities and are encouraged to communicate with both staff and each other during this time. In the main house the mornings are devoted to educational and social skills and the afternoons, from two until six o'clock, mainly to sport and some group activities. All the students attend the local sports centre and also practise other forms of sport such as riding, swimming or cycling.

After the evening meal the students have appropriate domestic tasks and hobbies to do under the sort of general staff supervision that their public school peers would recognise as supervised 'prep'. The evening drop in staff/student ratio to one to seven ensures that students work independently and have a fair amount of friendly contact with the other students in their shared bedrooms. Most students appear to be in bed by nine o'clock and there is little communal evening social activity during the week. The exception being birthday parties which are always held in the evening when there is a special meal of the student's choice, birthday cake, dancing and games. The student concerned plans the party, shops for the extra foods such as crisps etc, bakes the cake and organises the games. This gives every student the experience of throwing a party on their own birthday. Television, regarded as a 'time waster', is not watched during the week and only a very few selected programmes are allowed at the weekend. The majority of students have their own personal radio/stereo systems and no restriction is put on the use of these, so long as they are used with discretion and not played at full blast to disturb other students and staff.

THE WENTWOOD WEEK

The weekly and daily timetable remained much the same over the ten years and ensured that the expectation of every student would be to participate in working day that lasted from 9am-6pm, with one hour for lunch. They worked in 'groups' from 9am to 1pm, consisting of four students who would work with a member of staff in the relevant teaching subject. Lunch would be from 1pm-2pm and would have been prepared and cleared away by whichever group were working on that social skill.

From 2pm to 6pm students also worked in groups with the four members of staff on duty.

On Monday two members of staff would take ordinary group work while the other two would take half the students riding for the first part of the afternoon and then bring them back and take the other half riding. The groups left behind would probably be involved in gardening, woodwork or house maintenance depending on the special skills of the staff on duty. On Monday afternoons groups usually worked on money, language and literacy sessions. All areas of the timetable were accorded the same weight and were regarded as work by the students whether they were taught in the building or (more usually) participating in shopping and travel lessons in the town.

Group sessions were held on Tuesday mornings and everybody walked or cycled to the sports centre in the afternoon. They returned for group sessions from 5pm to 6pm during which one group would be preparing the evening meal. Wednesday followed a similar pattern with all the students going swimming from 5pm to 7pm at the local baths. Thursday afternoon included a special session of group movement for all the students which involved five participating members of staff. Sport was regarded not as a playtime but as a deliberate structured educational activity, with five staff involved every afternoon.

Friday's particular activity was a session of language and literacy in which every student wrote a letter home, regardless of their level of proficiency. Students who had achieved reasonable typing skills used the typewriters with help; those that could write a little, wrote by hand with help; and those who as yet could do neither, dictated their letters home. The words were often drawn out of them with great difficulty. Typing was a special subject on the curriculum and regarded as most important in that it provided every student with a standardised form of communication that could equal those of their more intelligent peers. Every student sent at least one piece of typing home a term, whatever their standard. The letters were supervised by HR, who was in charge of this particular activity and knew whether students had said similar things the week before. She insisted that they used a fair amount of communication skills to remember and relate the week's activities in a way that would be interesting to their families. The students' main topic when left to themselves was food, but if they really insisted on this area they would be encouraged to describe the fact that their home-grown cabbage came from their own garden or that they had actually been shopping themselves for it. By the end of the two years many students were capable of writing long and interesting letters home.

Life in the Grove, where students spent the final part of their two-year course, was less rigid and in the ten years covered by this study only three students failed to proceed to this final area of the course. Part of the day was often spent participating in a work experience scheme and rather more time was given to the running of the house. These students were encouraged to be virtually self-sufficient and make the majority of their own decisions as to food, shopping and financial budgeting. They also had a greater say in the use of their leisure time and where possible attended local community clubs in the evenings or weekends alongside the general public. They still attended the morning meeting and some academic-type lessons with students in the main house and always participated in the afternoon sports group sessions. Taking their turn in the rota they had to shop for, prepare and cook the ingredients for all their meals and also wash up afterwards – which made for a hectic schedule if they were to be ready for the statutory two o'clock return to work. The early bedtime still applied to the Grove but there were signs in 1990 of a more relaxed approach to watching the occasional early evening television programme. Many of the students came from homes where the television was on for most of the day with meals merely punctuating the transmission rather than halting it.

TRAINING FOR LEISURE

Probably the most effective way to illustrate the teaching of such an integrated curriculum is to take the particular example of training for leisure activities. Before students were able to benefit from neighbourhood leisure facilities, they had to learn how to travel by foot, bicycle or public transport to the required destination. Travel, which obviously also comprised road safety, was a particular interest of HR, who always taught this subject herself. The aim was to ensure that all students would have travel as part of their life repertoire. This would have both social advantages and lessen the burden of the carers usually responsible for this problem in the life of adults with learning disabilities. The ultimate aim in the Wentwood context was that all students should travel independently to and from Wentwood each term. In the ten years in question no student had ever travelled independently before they arrived at Wentwood, most had never even walked up the street without their mother. In the light of their previous experience parents took some persuasion to agree that such independence could be possible. The result of this teaching was that some terms every student left Wentwood and travelled, at least part of way, on their own. The more advanced students completed the entire journey home while the beginners, as a preliminary exercise, would travel the six miles to Devizes to be met by their parents.

Just one of many case histories serves to illustrate the efficacy of the teaching and the eventual generalisation of these learned skills. The parents of one very overprotected Down's syndrome student finally reluctantly accepted that she was competent to travel to London by coach quite independently. Accepting HR's advice, they met her at Park Lane for the first few journeys and showed her how to catch a connecting bus to Golders Green, gradually standing back and observing her from a distance to be certain she could cope with the transfer. Finally she was allowed to travel the entire complicated journey home from Melksham quite unsupervised. On one particular journey she arrived at the correct bus stop without realising there was a bus strike. She waited – and waited – and after about three-quarters of an hour asked somebody why there were no buses. On being told of the strike she telephoned her father (a learned Wentwood response to an emergency) and said she would get a taxi home. This she did. The principal's delighted response when informed of this incident at the start of the next term was not directed towards the student, who was already deemed competent in travel skills by the college, but towards the parents who confidently allowed their daughter to make her own decisions.

When referring to this type of incident HR termed it 'the outside of the book' – i.e. the edited version. The inside of the book was her meticulous teaching approach which involved parents from the very beginning. The first exercise in the curriculum was to teach the students to travel to the nearest pleasant place where they could take their parents out for a pub lunch. When parents came to visit the college to discuss various aspects of a student's development and future plans, it was automatically assumed that at the end of the session the student would then take them out to lunch using a bus to get to their destination. They were told to allow time for this extended visit. Parents would leave the premises having no idea of where they were going, with only the student knowing the final destination. Staff said they could see the worry and unease in the parent's walk as they left the college. Unknown to the parent and in case of emergencies, the student always had the plans for the day in a pocket. Parents would be taken by bus to a nearby National Trust village to sightsee and then go for a pub lunch, eventually returning to Wentwood by bus. On the next visit they would go further afield and eventually the student would phone the parents and make quite independent arrangements to take them out. They would meet in Bath which was a yet more complex expedition. Over ten years every student (bar two) eventually managed this progression.

TEACHING LEISURE SKILLS

As ever, the teaching consisted of doing and then talking about it afterwards. Four students would first go on a bus ride round the town while the principal observed their behaviour. The next phase was to board the bus together but allow one of the group to complete the journey alone while being followed by car or on foot. An expensive and time-consuming part of these travel exercises was the need for member of staff, with a watchful eye, to follow by car. Members of staff often preceded the student to a destination such as a bus station, to observe more complex travel behaviour. Students also had to master the speech requirements of unaccompanied travel which was no mean achievement for people with so little linguistic competence.

The students would then return to the classroom where they used a toy bus to practise the relevant behaviours. If their speech was not adequate for role play then a tape recorder was used to help them practise, with the HR taking the roles of bus driver/conductor. The lesson started with the students being made aware of the self-help skills necessary before going out, such as going to the toilet; doing up their flies; looking in the mirror; finding money; taking medication and checking that they had the list of things needed to go on a journey. Earlier road safety lessons were recapped and students learned the Wentwood way of asking for a ticket; asking for directions; whom to ask and where to go in an emergency to telephone Wentwood. Train journeys were also included in the syllabus and the more advanced students studied the local bus system, using timetables and transport-service maps to appreciate the relative distances of familiar places.

The ultimate test in the travel course came after students had fully mastered the intricacies of travel to and from the nearby city of Bath. When they were able to find a particular shop or cafe, where HR would meet them, they were each invited to find their way from Wentwood to her own home in Bath to join her for lunch. This journey was deliberately not included in the training programme and involved changing buses in the bus station, having first asked which bus to take to get to the destination. The address was only written down in cases of severe speech impediment. Having travelled from Wentwood to the bus station in Bath, the student then had to catch a small city minibus and ask where to get off. Having got off at the correct stop, it was necessary to ask for directions to the house. (The author can validate the difficulty of this particular journey having got lost in a similar attempt by car.) All the students over the ten years managed to complete this journey (dressed in their best clothes as befitted such a special occasion) where they were rewarded by a favourite lunch of their own choice. They were also warned that if they didn't manage the journey and the principal had to turn out to find them, they would not get their lunch. In ten years no student missed their lunch even though some were a little late!

In her travel lessons with the students part of the curriculum included learning to ask for directions from strangers. To demonstrate this aspect she used videoed scenes of friends of her own children (who the current students didn't know) asking for directions to the sports centre and other venues in the correct manner. The video was shown to the students who then had to go out and repeat the exercise in the same location using the same words. Students were informed that they wouldn't be videoed until they carried out the complete behavioral sequence in the correct manner. Videoing the students making fools of themselves seemed in this situation a singularly inappropriate way of teaching and merely reinforced the students' mistakes; whereas to use it as a reward for correct learning seemed a more positive approach.

A factor to be considered in video teaching was that the students often didn't relate to strangers in the more complex behavioral situations. The video, of necessity, used crowd observation techniques which students found confusing with no familiar cues to which they could relate. For example, when trying to teach students the correct way to join a queue in the post office or similar situation, if they were asked to analyse the behaviour of a woman in a red coat to see if she was standing well or badly etc, they failed to relate to or define the situation. If someone they knew by name and were familiar with was filmed standing in the same queue, preferably someone the same age from the local school, then the students identified the salient aspects of the behaviour being taught, quickly and with interest. In this context the widely used MENCAP 'Let's Go' films meant little to the students, proving useless until the students had experienced the activity in question. Wentwood reversed the usual procedure with this series by going out and experiencing the activity and then using the film as a basis for discussion.

Students were also taught not to approach strangers for information but always to approach either someone in uniform, or in an obvious position of authority such as behind a counter. If this was not possible they were taught to ask women with either children or shopping bags.

PHYSICAL EXERCISE

The effect of physical exercise on students' general development was of particular interest to HR who considered the effect of walking to be far the most beneficial. As such she gave it a special place in Wentwood life. Without the necessary physical abilities most students would be unable to participate in the leisure opportunities on offer. Many regular and routine practices at Wentwood evolved from the needs of particular students. Early in the development of the curriculum, Wentwood acquired a couple of 'lumpy' students that were unable to keep up with the others on the regular outdoor travel, shopping, post office and library trips. Teaching staff found this a problem and the other students in the group suffered as a consequence. In trying to solve this problem she started to take the two slow students out on regular shopping trips and walks and soon found by making up a game of brisk walking round the town they could improve their stamina. These trips took place on a daily basis first thing in the morning and proceeded at what she considered was 'a decent social pace'. The spin off appeared to be (as she had long suspected) that this exercise was successful in improving both their bodies and their minds. This then became a regular part of the curriculum and she always took new students walking first thing every morning, with entirely beneficial effects. The rationale for placing Wentwood in the centre of a small market town was the ease with which students could walk to every place they needed to visit. Shops, doctors, dentists, clubs, sports centre, church and village hall were all within walking distance.

Cycling was another important feature of Wentwood life. Students were trained initially in the local school playground at the weekends, until they actually learned to ride. They then progressed to the small lanes in the square outside the college. Eventually students cycled to work experience and often cycled behind the minibus if it was too full on an outing.

The afternoons at the sports centre gave students the choice of a wide range of leisure activities. Having previously assembled any special clothes or equipment, they walked the one and three-quarter mile each way to and from the sports centre, accompanied by a member of staff. The walk went through the main street of the busy market town and involved negotiating a large dual-carriage trunk road carrying traffic heading for a nearby motorway. The centre offered a choice of activities and students were encouraged to sample all of them. They attended the public sessions and were responsible for changing their own clothes, showering and using the lockers and keys correctly alongside the general public.

WEEKEND LEISURE ACTIVITIES, EVENING CLASSES AND CLUBS

It was hoped that the concept of leisure would become part of the weekend and holiday lifestyle in the students' adult life. Cycling and horse riding were encouraged as weekend activities. With the help of a teacher with a particular interest in cycling, students joined in events with local cycling groups. The weekend activities were planned in some detail. Wentwood staff were aware that, left to themselves, students would fall into the usual inactivity which was a particular feature of their home lives. An added reason for HR seeing every student in the Friday letter writing session was part of a deliberate policy to keep both staff and students 'on their toes'. She expected every student to be able to tell her during the afternoon what they were planning to do at the weekend. This should have already been discussed and planned with the members of staff on weekend rota. Students were not allowed to be told by staff what to do during the weekend but were expected to plan these activities during the previous week. This anticipatory work towards weekend leisure was designed to overcome the inevitable weekend inactivity usually experienced by residents in group homes.

The local village hall/community centre displayed a list of all clubs, concerts and other activities on an outside notice board. Students were encouraged to find out about suitable weekend and evening activities listed on the board and attend with the general public. Several of the students attended the camera club and by using the local notice boards they also found out about the bazaars, jumble sales, films, exhibitions, coffee mornings and discos which are a feature of life in any neighbourhood community. In the summer, many picnics and walking trips were planned with great care. The students began to realise that the planned use of local transport could take them away from their current environment to somewhere more pleasant on a warm sunny day. An added incentive was the visit to a local pub and finishing the day with a meal in a cafe or restaurant.

All weekend activities were structured to take due regard of financial restraints, so that students would realise that the relative cost of some activities make them unsuitable on a regular basis for people living on the type of income they will eventually have to budget for themselves. It was hoped to provide an extended repertoire of outdoor and indoor activities. To aid this type of thinking the MENCAP 'Lets Go' series of slides produced by Brian Rix were frequently shown as a starting point for discussion. This type of weekend activity was a considerable challenge to students who have spent their formative years watching sport and films on the television at weekends.

At various times over the years Wentwood has introduced students to evening classes in an attempt to involve them in leisure activities after the working day. Typing was initially started as an evening class where students would go to a neighbour who taught typing in her own home. Two students went in rotation after supper from 7pm to 9pm with an able student taking a more dependent student. Before attending classes all the students had to wash themselves and change their clothes and ensure that they were clean and tidy after the day's work. Gateway Clubs were also visited in the evenings but the staff had reservations about the students using a facility solely for people with learning disabilities, rather than the excellent local facilities. Several students attended St John's Ambulance Brigade evening classes which entailed wearing a complex uniform which they had to cope with by themselves. One student joined a local swimming club which involved a member of staff having to collect him at 11pm. The Girls Brigade, Venture Scouts and the local youth club were also local evening activities that students attended as regular members. Initially students were accompanied by a member of Wentwood staff who in exchange would offer some input into the organisation. As students became involved and integrated into the activities in their own right, this staff input was withdrawn. In all extra curricular activity the policy was for staff to teach students the correct behaviour and then withdraw. The policy continued as each new group of students joined an activity.

If students were unable to attend the various clubs independently after the requisite time then they were withdrawn. Community integration rather than community tolerance was the Wentwood aim. An example of this was the local keep-fit club where students were withdrawn after a term because they were unable to follow the verbal instructions quickly enough. Therefore they would never be able to cope successfully on their own. One or two students always attended local adult literacy classes. This was thought to be important as a social activity and would also make them aware of something else they could do on their own in any community. Although the students didn't need the service from a literacy point of view, their own classes being superior, it was used as an entry into the system. Wherever they then saw the book logo they would know they would be welcome to join in, thus extending their repertoire of things to do in their free time.

COMMUNITY LIFE

During their leisure time at weekends and in the evenings, there were several other extensions of college life into the wider community. Students participated in the 'clean up Melksham scheme' regularly instituted by the Rotary club. This was merely an extension of their outside maintenance and gardening group work and gave the students a practical generalisation of their often tedious and repetitive college experience. Wentwood regularly assumed responsibility for two streets in the annual Red Cross flag day and staff were insistent that this task was carried out in exactly the same way by the students as by the general public in the other streets. For many years the college was also involved in the Kennett and Avon canal scheme and from the early days of the college, students regularly attended with a member of staff who was involved in the reclamation work. All these community activities were carried out by very small numbers of students at any one time. Wentwood had no wish to overwhelm the local community with an obvious presence.

HOLIDAYS

Wentwood particularly stressed Bank Holiday outings and hoped to train the students to use their leisure time effectively so that at Bank Holidays, and other times when their ATC or college of further education are closed, they will be aware of the opportunities for recreation in their own environment.

An extension of the integrated P-A-C approach was the annual term-time holiday which all the students took in small groups. The planning started well ahead with maps, pictures and lists of things to take with them appearing on the dining room notice board some weeks in advance of the holiday. Students were involved in all the usual travel and accommodation bookings and routes were planned in detail. They travelled to their holiday destination unaccompanied using the public coach service. When they finally arrived at their destination they had an excellent opportunity to generalise all their previous leisure learning skills to a totally new environment.

The final-year independent Grove students were expected to take rather more responsibility on their holiday and each student assumed responsibility for one day's catering. They were expected to arrive with a whole day's menus prepared, so that they could shop locally for the ingredients. They were expected to prepare the food, unaided, in a strange kitchen. Last year everybody coped well with this exercise, except the least efficient student who opted for a pub meal which was enthusiastically supported by the other students – and endorsed as a realistic choice by the staff!

Parents were kept fully informed about the student's progress on the holiday and invited to visit the students for a day, joining in with the activities. It was hoped that this experience would encourage both parents and students to implement a more independent life style at home during the Wentwood holidays.

UTILISING LEISURE TRAINING IN WORK EXPERIENCE

Although Wentwood stress that the college is running a pre-vocational course, it is nevertheless thought appropriate to give students some experience of a working day. This becomes another opportunity to generalise domestic and leisure skills learned in the Wentwood context, to a wider setting. Work experience also allows the students to realise that the unremitting toil involved in real work can be boring and requires great attention.

All students, regardless of sex, are taught simple gardening, horticulture, wood-work, house maintenance, domestic cleaning, cooking, laundry and all the various additional skills needed to run two large houses and gardens with no outside paid staff. This makes for a considerably more realistic life style than is provided in most local authority group homes. Wentwood students can see an added point of the rigid programmed teaching of these areas when they are able to use them in a genuine work experience project in the wider community. However, there was another aspect of work experience Wentwood felt they had to build into some part of the course, enabling the students to have an extended experience of sheer solid directed group labour every day for two weeks. It was felt that students must learn that work was not just a treat that took them out of Wentwood a day a week, but that it went on and on and on.

Once a year the college found a genuine project work experience within the grounds. One year it was taking down and building a new greenhouse; another year the redecoration of two rooms; the next year building a patio etc. For this exercise, two groups of four students and two members of staff were taken out of the Wentwood timetable completely and worked on the job from 9am to 5pm every day. They became quite separate from the Wentwood routine, missing lessons, sports and both the fun and the tedium of their everyday lives. The students made their own sandwiches the night before. Dressed in overalls with the statutory thermos flask, they were ready to start work at 9am each morning. After finishing at 5pm, they showered and were able to rest, until the others finished group activities before joining them for the evening meal.

Two or three days into this novel experience the students invariably decided they had had enough! They would get tired, cold, or wet and decide they would prefer to go riding or visit the sports centre. Grumbling would be endemic and the staff concerned took a very tough approach, insisting the work continued. Other staff would visit the project, taking photographs of progress and heaping praise on the students. This would help them to get through this stage and begin to experience the pleasure of completing a task which left a tangible record for everyone to see. At the end of the two weeks they knocked off at mid-day on the final Friday and had a celebratory lunch with the principal at the local pub. a photograph album was compiled of the various stages of the completed work and the trustees of Wentwood would personally visit the project and thank the students. By the end of this time not only had the students learned about work, but the staff had also learned just which student was capable of sustained work. They were often surprised which students could and could not cope.

THE CHURCH

The church was also an important part of Wentwood life and several studies now show that one of the few agencies to facilitate community integration of the devel-opmentally disabled is the church. As with all other practices, Wentwood tried to instil habits at first, until students were aware enough of the concept to be able to make informed choices. They were only allowed to choose when their behavioral skills were adequate for them to carry out such a choice successfully. All students were expected to attend the church of their own denomination on Sundays. The organisation of this was considerable, as students often went to as many as five different churches in the town, one of which adjoined the Grove. They would go with whichever staff was on duty and whose church it was. If this was not possible, Wentwood would appeal to a church to find someone to initially be responsible for the student and then gradually reduce the dependence. As the church habit became instilled, inquiries would be made of Wentwood parents as to why particular students had not for example, made their first communion, been confirmed, had their barmitzvah etc. Eventually there were groups of students attending local confirmation groups, first communion Catholic groups, Baptist and Congregational teachings as part of the local church congregations. A social spin off was that as students went round the town on their daily lessons and social activities, total strangers to the staff would know the student from church. This enabled the student to have their own tiny part of community individuality, quite separate from the Wentwood world. Staff would go to great lengths to ensure that students attended church social functions even if this meant missing part of a day's group lesson or activity. The church was seen as a very suitable area where students could develop their own individuality, personal relationships and self-importance.

This emphasis on church attendance had a particularly beneficial effect on parents, many of whom revealed their own religious 'hang ups'. Although not themselves ostensibly practising any religious beliefs, they had felt that their child could never be a Christian (or whatever faith they subscribed to) because he was mentally handicapped. The fact that as an independent student their child was having a similar religious upbringing to that given to his siblings, appeared to be a tremendous relief to many parents. This often brought out religious practices in the parents that they had put aside because they had felt they couldn't share the experience as a family any more. Many families reverted back to regular church attendance in the holiday times with their student offspring. Difficulties arose with various non-believing staff who could only see it as a religious exercise but they were finally convinced of the benefit to the student in the areas of social and personal development. Churchgoing could be seen as a valid weekend activity.

Selected Bibliography

Brechin, A. and Walmsley J. (eds) (1989) *Making Connections: Reflecting on the Lives and Experiences of People with Learning Difficulties*. London: Hodder and Stoughton.

Brown, R.I., Bayer, M.B. and Brown, P.M. (1992) *Empowerment and Developmental Handicaps: Choices and Quality of Life*. London: Chapman and Hall.

Felce, D. (1989) *The Andover project: staffed housing for adults with severe or profound mental handicaps*. Kidderminster: BIMH Publications

Felce, D. and Togood S. (1988) *Close to Home: a local housing service and its impact on the lives of nine adults with severe and profound mental handicaps*. Kidderminster: BIMH Publications.

Firth, H. and Rapley, M. (1990) *From Acquaintance to Friendship: Issues for people with learning disabilities*. Kidderminster: BIMH.

Gunzburg, H.C. *P-A-C: (Progress Assessment Chart)* – various forms. London: RSMHC (MENCAP)

King's Fund Centre (1980) *An Ordinary Life: Comprehensive Locally-based Residential Services for Mentally Handicapped People*. London: King's Fund Centre.

Rose-Ackerman, S.(1982) 'Mental retardation and society: the ethics and politics of normalisation.' *Ethics 93*, 81–101.

Seed, P. and Kaye, G. (1994) *Handbook for Assessing and Managing Care in the Community*. London: Jessica Kingsley Publishers.

Shalock, R.L. (ed) (1990) *Quality of Life: Perspectives and Issues*. Washington: American Association on Mental Retardation.

Sinson, J.C. (1992) 'A Sixth Form College for Mentally Handicapped Adolescents.' 'Wentwood Education – an Analysis of Environmental, social and Educational Assessments.' 'Personalisation through Social Education.' In H.C. Gunzburg (ed) 'Despite Mental Handicap'. Monograph: *The British Journal of Developmental Disabilities*.

Sinson, J.C. (1993) *Group Homes and Community Integration of Developmentally Disabled People: Micro-Institutionalisation?* London: Jessica Kingsley Publishers.

Stainton, C.L.S. (1992) 'Monitoring Progress – Wentwood Statistical Analysis.' In H.C. Gunzburg (ed) 'Despite Mental Handicap.' Monograph: *The British Journal of Developmental Disabilities*.